What's That Rash?

How to identify and treat
childhood rashes

What's That Rash?

How to identify and treat
childhood rashes

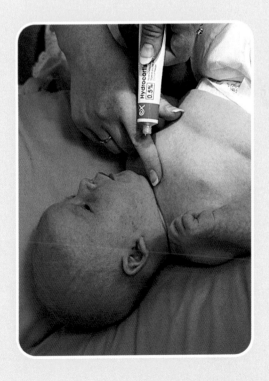

CHANCELLOR
PRESS

Prisca Middlemiss

Part of the **MYRiAD** series

First published in Great Britain in 2002
by Hamlyn, a division of
Octopus Publishing Group Ltd

This edition published in 2010 by Chancellor Press,
an imprint of Octopus Publishing Group Ltd
Endeavour House,
189 Shaftesbury Avenue,
London WC2H 8JY
www.octopusbooks.co.uk

An Hachette UK Company
www.hachette.co.uk

ISBN: 978-0-753719-75-6

A CIP catalogue record for this book is available
from the British Library

Printed and bound in China

Note

This book is not intended as a
substitute for personal medical
advice. The reader should consult a
physician in all matters relating to
health and particularly in respect of
any symptoms which may require
diagnosis or medical attention.
While the advice and information
are believed to be accurate and true
at the time of going to press,
neither the author nor the publisher
can accept any legal responsibility
or liability for any errors or
omissions that may be made.

Contents

Colour coding

Newborn and babies

Rashes with fever

Rashes spread by skin contact

Non-contagious rashes

Introduction

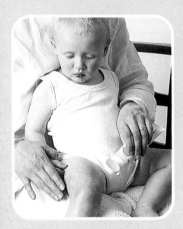

This book tells you what the most common skin complaints and rashes in children are like. If your child has a rash, you will be able to use it to help you decide whether you can treat the child at home. It tells you when it's important to get medical advice and how quickly you need to react.

The pictures will help you to identify your child's rash. But, although some rashes point very clearly to a cause, others are more perplexing. To help with identification, the book tells you how common the rash is and what it's most often confused with.

Many rashes can be simply treated at home. The book tells you how, using simple remedies such as cooling. It also tells you when it's appropriate to use creams and medicines that you can buy from a pharmacy.

Some rashes need medical attention. The book tells you when to seek a doctor's diagnosis and what you can expect that treatment to involve.

Some entries also have information on complementary therapies. Treating rashes with complementary remedies isn't always appropriate, although some people use these remedies widely. Sometimes there is good research to support the use of complementary medicines, for eczema, for example. Sometimes there is just a lot of accumulated expertise, but little or no research. Always ask your child's doctor before using a complementary therapy. When you consult a doctor, tell them of any complementary treatments that you have used.

Important:
This book should never take the place of a doctor's advice or care. Babies and young children can become ill very fast. In particular you should always contact a doctor or call your emergency medical number if:

- There is a rash that does not fade when pressed with a see-through glass.
- The child has a fever of 40°C (104°F) or more.
- There is any swelling of the face, lips or mouth or any difficulty swallowing.
- The rash makes your baby uncomfortable or itchy, or it's very extensive.
- The rash is weeping or spots get infected.
- There are other signs of illness such as noisy or difficult breathing or refusing drinks or unusual lifelessness or sleepiness.

Preventing skin conditions

Most children have smooth, unblemished skin of a softness that's a special feature of childhood. The conditions that they suffer from are most often temporary and frequently self-healing. As they have a whole cluster of causes, it's rarely possible to prevent them. Sometimes it isn't even desirable. Most families are happy for an otherwise healthy child to catch chickenpox. It's one nasty but necessary childhood experience to tick off the list, like the first haircut or the first day at school. One attack of chickenpox almost always confers lifelong immunity and for most children – although not all – it is a mild disease.

Even skin conditions that you might associate with poor hygiene, such as scabies or headlice, are in fact just as common in clean children.

Where skin conditions run in the family – if you are affected or your partner is – you'll be especially concerned to do what you can to protect your child. Sometimes it's possible, but often either it's not possible or would cause such an upheaval in your life that it isn't worth the effort.

ABOVE: Children should shower thoroughly after swimming. In hard water areas, young children may need to moisturize sensitive skin after showering as chemicals in domestic water (including chlorine and calcium) can act as irritants.

All that being said, there are simple steps that you can take to stop your child getting some skin conditions and, most importantly, to stop early conditions in their tracks:

- **Daily all-over wash or bath.** Stops some bacteria from multiplying unchecked, cleans again danger spots such as the nappy area and lets you pick up early signs of problems, such as dryness.

- **Use the simplest products you can buy.** Young skin is best washed with plain water. Cleansers are needed only for skin that gets dirty. As young skin is also sensitive, it's best to choose products without fragrances or preservatives. This is especially important if a rash has already developed because the affected skin is extra sensitive.

- **Reduce chemicals** in direct contact with your child's skin. Rinse well after swimming; don't use fabric conditioner.

- **Reduce irritants.** Some skin conditions (such as warts or cold sores) start by a virus entering damaged skin. Keeping irritation to a minimum lessens the chance of damage, so clothes and bedding should be soft (synthetics are as good as cotton).

- **Keep temperatures even.** Extremes of cold and particularly of heat exacerbate many skin conditions.

- **Take rapid steps to stop scratching.** Itchy conditions often become infected this way. Use soothing creams and calamine on the itchy areas and antihistamine medicines by mouth to disrupt the itch–scratch cycle.

- **Moisturize dry skin.** Many skin conditions (such as eczema) can be completely controlled by keeping your child's skin really well moisturized.

- **Don't allow sogginess.** Warm, moist skin encourages fungal growth, especially in skin creases. Keep feet and nappy area as dry as possible.

- **Sunlight helps** conditions such as psoriasis and to a lesser extent eczema. Obviously, you must protect your child from sunburn.

- **Salt and sea water** are antiseptic and can help weeping eczema.

Immunization

The best way to protect a child against certain infections that cause a rash and fever is by immunization. Now that vaccines are offered routinely, in the year 2000 in England and Wales only 74 people caught measles, yet in pre-vaccine days, it used to lay low hundreds of thousands of children. In the same year, a mere nine children caught German measles (rubella). The numbers of children catching the C strains of meningitis fell to an all-time low after the introduction in 1999 of the Men C vaccine. Immunization against Hib (Haemophilus influenzae b) infection, which can cause meningitis as well as a range of other serious illnesses, cut the number of affected pre-school children to 66 in the year 2000.

Side effects?

One effect of immunization is to make once common rashes so rare that doctors almost never see them and medical students only learn about them from pictures. This impacts on their diagnostic accuracy, so that the vast majority of children suspected of having measles or German measles actually don't. In the year 2000, in England and Wales less than four per cent of the people suspected by doctors of having measles really had it. For German measles, diagnostic accuracy was even lower – just one per cent of people with suspected rubella really had that infection. Of course the other thing this demonstrates is how difficult it is to diagnose rashes.

Vaccines are also available against pneumococcal disease, which can cause septicaemia and meningitis, and, in the USA, against chickenpox. But it's not all a success story. A vaccine against the B strains of meningococcal meningitis has proved elusive. The health departments in the Netherlands have developed a vaccine that has gone through trials with some success on babies. To work well, however, it needs more than the standard three doses. Now this vaccine is being developed further, both as a stand-alone immunization and linked with a pneumococcal vaccine.

Infection	Vaccine?	UK	USA
Chickenpox	Varicella	No	Yes
Measles	MMR*	Yes	Yes
Meningitis and septicaemia			
Hib infection	Hib	Yes	Yes
Group B disease (Meningococcal)	Under development		
Group C disease (Meningococcal)	Men C	Yes	No
Pneumococcal disease	Prevenar	At-risk children only	Yes
Rubella	MMR*	Yes	Yes

Note: A vaccine available in the USA against Lyme disease is only for use in adults, not children.
*MMR contains measles, mumps and rubella viruses.

School rules

Some skin conditions can be caught either by direct contact with the spots or blisters or by breathing in infected droplets from someone who is ill. Schools and nurseries may expect you to keep a child with a skin condition at home until he or she is no longer infectious. School exclusion rules are drawn up with advice from the local consultant in communicable disease. But some schools follow outdated practices and exclude children for longer than is needed or for illnesses that cannot be controlled by keeping children at home.

The guidelines that follow are based on evidence from research studies and are published by the Public Health Laboratory Service for England and Wales. School rules in other countries may differ slightly.

A child with the following conditions should not go to school:

Skin condition	How long for?	Further advice
Chickenpox	5 days from start of rash.	None.
Impetigo	Until sores have crusted over and healed.	None.
Measles	5 days from start of rash.	None.
Meningitis	Until child is completely better.	Close contacts are given antibiotics as protection.
Rubella	5 days from start of rash.	None.
Scabies	Until child has been treated.	None.
Scarlet fever	Once treated, 5 days.	None.

Infections for which no exclusion is recommended:
Children with these infectious illnesses and conditions are allowed to come to school so long as they feel well.

Illness or condition	Reasons
Cold sores	Virtually all children have already been infected.
Hand, foot and mouth disease	Not a serious illness; most infectious before rash comes out.
Headlice	Headlice spread anyway. The child should be treated, however, using the approach recommended locally.
Lyme disease	People do not catch it from each other.
Molluscum	Not a serious condition; not very infectious between schoolchildren.
Ringworm	Not a serious infection; not very infectious.
Roseola	Not a serious illness; usually affects children under nursery age.
Slapped cheek disease	Only infectious before rash comes out.
Verrucas	Risk of infection is presumed to be low.

Baby massage

After the birth of a baby, mothers feel an overwhelmingly protective urge to be in skin-to-skin contact through the largest and most sensitive organ of the body.

Research has shown that mothers first touch their new baby's hands and feet with their fingertips; within minutes they start stroking the body with the palm. Touching the skin, it seems, is an instinctive way to get to know a baby.

ABOVE: Massaged babies are more relaxed, sleep and feed better and suffer less from colic. Premature babies put on weight faster. It's uncertain why, but lower stress levels, better sleep and stimulation to the immune system all probably play their part.

Touch and massage have important therapeutic implications for older children too. Children with skin conditions can feel disliked and rejected if, as all too often happens, other children will not touch them or even hold hands. Feeling unwelcome is one of the greatest social handicaps. Massage overcomes that sense of rejection.

In countries where water has been traditionally in short supply, oil massage takes the place of washing.

There is no right or wrong way to massage. So long as you are sensible, massaging in a warm room and starting only when the baby is alert and contented – but not just after a feed – you can follow your instincts. The younger the baby, the more important it is to use a simple oil, such as a mineral-based baby oil, almond oil or olive oil.

Here are two ways to massage:

1 Lay the baby on a warmed towel on the floor or stretch the towel over your outstretched legs and put your baby on his back, facing

RIGHT: Parents say that massaged babies respond faster to being comforted. So massage may be especially important for babies with sore or itchy skin conditions.

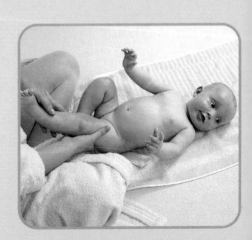

ABOVE: Massage oil should be gently warmed in the palm of the hand before starting. Baby massage has a doubly relaxing effect, de-stressing both mother and infant.

Massage oil for an older baby

Almond oil or a 4:1 mix of almond and jojoba, to which is added a drop or two of rose, neroli, lavender or Roman camomile.

ABOVE: Even young babies' feet can be ticklish, so when massaging, use a firm, gentle pressure.

you. Remove his clothes and with a little oil on the palm of each hand, run your hands from his ankles to the tops of his legs and then lightly down again. Massage each foot three or four times in either direction using your thumb. Using the palm of one hand, very lightly massage his abdomen in a clockwise direction. Gently glide your hands up and round the shoulders, then down the arms to the wrists and back again to the shoulders. Repeat this three or four times. If your baby is still perfectly content, turn him onto his tummy and massage the backs of his legs, moving your hands lightly upwards to his bottom. Then run your hands in parallel up the spine to his neck, down round his shoulders to his sides and back to his bottom. Leave his hands unmassaged and don't massage his face in case oil gets into his eyes or mouth.

2 Starting at the groin, run your hands down the legs to the soles of the feet, then up to the legs, thighs, the abdomen, the shoulders and the arms. Starting with the palms, gently massage the hands and arms. Then turn your baby onto his stomach, and lightly massage the calves, the backs of the thighs, the buttocks and the back. Finally massage the scalp very gently. The entire session should last around 5–7 minutes.

Black skin

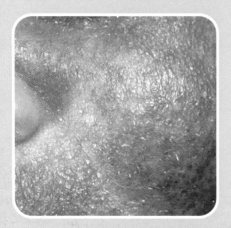

Black skin is naturally shiny, because it produces more sweat and sebum than white skin. In a cool, northern climate, however, it can turn noticeably dry and scaly, making it look grey and ashy. The use of emollients (moisturizer for medically diagnosed dry skin or eczema) and coconut oil will protect it against dry-skin conditions such as eczema.

ABOVE: Protecting young children against dry-skin conditions like eczema (above) is easier in cultures where an oily look to the skin is acceptable. Greasier preparations like ointments and paraffin are useful, as well as refined cocoa and shea butter.

People with black and white skin have the same number of skin colour cells, called melanocytes. However, in black people the cells produce more colour more responsively than in white people. This means that black skin is more protective against sunlight, although it also means that it tends to produce dark marks after any injury or inflammation. Frequently the skin darkens, but sometimes it lightens instead. Fortunately, these colour changes are usually temporary but they can take many months to return to normal.

Infected eczema, impetigo, chickenpox, contact dermatitis, insect bites and pityriasis can all leave the skin looking temporarily darker. Nappy rash and seborrhoeic dermatitis can leave it paler. Any itchy skin condition that makes a child scratch is likely to lead to temporary blemishes and colour changes, so it is particularly important to get medical treatment early on to prevent damage and long-term colour changes. However, steroid creams can themselves produce temporary skin colour

changes, so they need to be used under supervision.

Black skin is not only different in colour to white skin, it also reacts differently to damage. Children with black skin are more likely than children with white skin to be left with obvious scars. Scars not only produce more fibrous tissue, but the tissue has a tendency to grow beyond the site of the original injury and form lumps known as keloids. Even a relatively mild rash such as chickenpox can leave a dark-skinned child with keloid scarring. Although silicone gel sheets help to flatten the scars, they have to be kept in contact with the skin for many weeks.

Dermatologists usually advise parents to consider carefully before allowing their child to undergo any procedure that could damage the skin, in particular ear piercing. However, many parents believe that procedures carried out in babyhood are less likely to cause keloids than in later childhood.

It is also important to distinguish between skin that has lost some pigment after an inflammatory

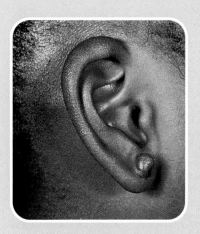

illness but will recover, and the totally depigmented skin of vitiligo (see page 67). Black skin that's damaged or repeatedly scratched also tends to thicken and coarsen, forming deep cracks. This can be very obvious in children with eczema.

Skin conditions themselves look different depending on skin colour. The redness of inflammation in a white skin turns a black skin purplish-brown. If any redness is visible it is a more serious sign than in a child with white skin. Rashes can look quite different, with spots involving the hair follicles being much more common in dark-skinned children with eczema or pityriasis rosea.

Conditions that appear more common in black children include atopic eczema, perhaps because black skin dries out in a northern climate, and this often takes the form of discoid eczema. Ringworm on the scalp is especially common in children of African and Afro-Caribbean origin, for reasons that are unclear but may include hair styling methods.

However, some conditions are less common in black children of Afro-Caribbean origin, including psoriasis. Slapped cheek disease is believed to be less common, but that may be because it is hard to spot, as are viral rashes and purpura.

As changes in the appearance and texture of black skin are subtle and hard to spot, a parent's observations are especially valuable. Trust your instincts – a good doctor will listen to your concerns with particular care.

Newborn and babies

Diagnosis

Young babies have sensitive skin that is easily irritated. Working out what is wrong when a young or new baby has a rash is unquestionably the job of a health professional. Some rashes are hard to identify even for a doctor with an interest in, and many years of experience of, dermatology.

Although many rashes are minor, some are not. Young babies can become ill very quickly. If their skin is hot or inflamed, they lose heat and fluid even more quickly than an older baby or young child, and much more quickly than an adult.

People who are with a baby all the time can, however, watch them. Your observations are key information for the doctor, midwife or health visitor whom you consult.

If your young baby has a skin blemish or rash, ask yourself:
- Was he or she born with it?

- Where did you notice it first?

- How long has it been there?

- Does he or she seem unwell in any other way – more sleepy, floppy or hot than you expect?

- Is the rash unchanging, in one place? Is it spreading or moving?

- Does it come and go?

- Does it seem to bother your baby?

- Does anything seem to make it better or worse?

- Does anyone else in the family have skin problems?

For skin blemishes your baby was born with, see
Stork marks and Mongolian blue
    spots
Port wine stain
Strawberry mark
Moles

For rashes limited to the scalp, bottom or face, see
Baby acne
Cradle cap
Nappy rash
Milia
Seborrhoeic dermatitis

For rashes over the rest of the body, see
Dry skin
Heat rash
Seborrhoeic dermatitis
Erythema neonatorum
Scalded skin syndrome

Dry skin

What is it?
Dry skin is caused by loss of water through the normally protective barrier of sebum or oils. The sebum level may be reduced in some babies with an inherited tendency or it may be affected by cold, windy weather. Hot, dry, indoor atmospheres can dry skin unnaturally and some chemicals in soaps and bubble baths degrease the skin, dissolving the sebum layer. Unprotected skin is more likely to react to perfumes and chemicals and to develop patches of irritation.

Key signs
Roughened skin surface, sometimes with redness and tiny cracks developing.

*** Very common.

Symptoms
- Roughness, especially in exposed skin such as cheeks.
- If cracks develop, the skin may become very sore.
- May have inflammation and redness.

What to do
- At the first sign of dryness, smooth on an emollient moisturizing cream or aqueous cream liberally.
- Use a soap substitute.
- Check the diagnosis with your health visitor or doctor.

Medical treatment
If your doctor believes your baby's dry skin is caused by eczema, she will prescribe an emollient for the dryness and possibly a mild steroid cream for inflamed patches.

Outlook
Your baby may outgrow the tendency to dry skin. Meanwhile, you can do a lot to control it:
- Cover or moisturize a baby's face outdoors in a pushchair as raw wintry or windy weather makes it worse.

- Turn down central heating or open a window to avoid a dry, overheated environment at home.
- Avoid bubble baths and soaps as any detergent or soap that foams can strip the skin of its protective oily layer. Even soaking in hot water for too long washes away the protective film, letting water seep in and making the skin swell and wrinkle as if it's been under a sticking plaster too long. To preserve your baby's natural, silky feel, avoid using soaps and detergents.
- If water isn't enough on its own to clean your baby, use a lotion.
- Shower your baby thoroughly after swimming to wash off traces of chlorine.

Looks like
Atopic eczema (see pages 68–71).

Note
Children with black skin are prone to dryness. This gives the skin an ashy appearance, commonly between the fingers, on the elbows and legs. Massage twice daily with a moisturizer containing pure petroleum jelly, cocoa butter or shea butter.

Erythema neonatorum

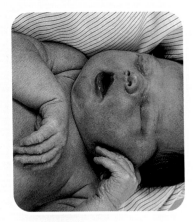

Key signs
Patchy red rash on newborn baby.

∗∗∗ Very common.

What is it?
A passing rash that commonly starts in the first two to four days after birth in babies born at term. Flat, uneven-shaped red patches of skin appear, sometimes quite dramatically, on the baby's trunk, arms and legs. Doctors do not yet understand the cause.

Symptoms
- Flat, red, blotchy rash.
- Spots range from tiny to 2–3cm (1in) across.
- Small clear blisters or yellow spots.
- Rash most obvious on the trunk; face, arms and nappy area can also be affected.
- Baby is otherwise well.

What to do
Consult your midwife or doctor. They are most likely to reassure you that the rash will fade in two to three days and that in the meantime it will cause the baby no discomfort.

No treatment is needed. Although the spots look infected, they are not.

Looks like
Virus infection.
Skin infection.

What else?
Affects half of all new babies but unusual in premature babies.

Also called erythema toxicum or urticaria neonatorum.

Milia in new babies

What is it?
Also known as 'milk rash', milia are small white or yellowish spots on a new baby's skin (usually over the face). They are caused by minute glands working overtime to produce the oily sebum that naturally waterproofs the skin. Excess production occurs when hormones transfer from mother to baby in late pregnancy. As the effect fades over the baby's first few weeks of life, the milia disappear without trace.

Symptoms
- Swathes of pinprick yellow spots on the face, forehead and nose.
- A light sprinkling of creamy-white spots on the face or body.

What to do
Leave them. Do nothing. Milia will disappear without trace. The white cysts will pop open and disappear within six weeks. Meanwhile, resist any temptation to squeeze milia because this can leave a scar.

Creamy white spots may be tiny cysts containing keratin, a fibrous protein that makes nails and is also found in the skin and hair.

Key signs
Crops of white or yellow spots on face of otherwise well baby.

*** Very common.

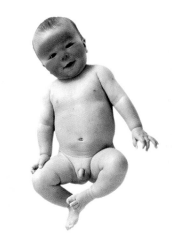

Scalded skin syndrome

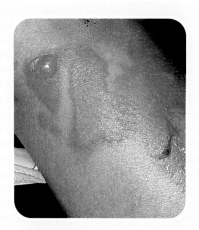

Key signs
Young baby whose skin
peels off, leaving a scalded
appearance.

∗ Uncommon.

Caution
Can be life threatening, so
seek urgent medical
attention.

What is it?
**A bacterial infection caused by a
staphylococcus spreads from its
original site, such as an umbilical
infection or an impetigo sore.
Toxins travel in the bloodstream to
the skin, causing the upper layer to
separate as if burnt.**

Scalded skin syndrome affects
babies variably and a serious attack
can be life threatening unless
treated promptly. Although it is
most common in young babies, it
can also affect young children or
people with under-functioning
immune systems.

Symptoms
- Reddened skin appears around
  crusted impetigo-like sores.
- Reddening spreads, skin feels
  tender and hot and may blister.
- The epidermis (outer skin layer)
  peels off in sheets to leave red,
  exposed tissues.
- Even touching and holding the
  child causes the skin to peel.
- Peeling affects any part of the
  body.
- Baby becomes feverish,
  uncomfortable and hard to settle.

What to do
- Early treatment is vital.
- If peeling has already started,
  cover the child in a layer of
  plastic film before laying a sheet
  over him or her.
- Give clear drinks.

Medical treatment
- Antibiotics are given by mouth if
  the infection is identified early, or
  by intravenous infusion.
- Further treatment is as for a child
  with burns: extra fluid input to
  balance loss through exposed
  skin, temperature regulation and
  skin protection to prevent further
  infection.
- Hospital treatment as for burns.

Outlook
Mild cases where the peeling is
superficial may clear naturally in a
week or two. With treatment,
healing takes five to seven days.

Baby acne

What is it?
An inflammatory skin disease affecting the sebaceous (oil, sebum-producing) glands associated with the tiny hair follicles on the face and other parts of the body. Under the influence of the mother's hormones, babies with acne over-produce the sebum that normally keeps the skin well oiled. As a result the hair follicle partly blocks, causing facial spots. In baby acne, these spots persist after the newborn period or develop later.

Key signs
Acne-like blackheads and spots on a baby's face, especially the cheeks.

∗ Uncommon.

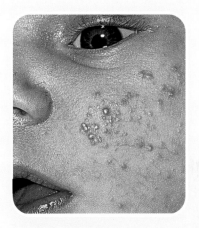

The spots are very similar to teenage acne, consisting of a mixture of blackheads, raised red spots, cysts and infected spots.

In addition to producing extra sebum, the sebaceous glands tend to become blocked by plugs of keratin, the protein part of the skin, creating blackheads. This can allow bacteria inside to multiply and inflame the surrounding skin.

Symptoms
- Red spots, appearing first on the face, especially the cheeks. Spots may develop into pustules with a white or yellowy head and can be painful.
- You often see whiteheads and blackheads (comedones).
- Spots usually first appear in babies aged three to six months.
- Baby acne is more common in boys.

What to do
Consult a doctor.

Medical treatment
The doctor can prescribe an antibiotic cream or lotion to cover the affected area.

Occasionally the doctor will suggest a course of oral antibiotics.

Outlook
Babies with darker skin types may have obvious changes in skin colour around the scars. These gradually disappear.

Children severely affected as babies should anticipate a return in adolescence.

Baby acne is very occasionally linked with a hormone disorder in which girls are exposed to masculinizing hormones.

Baby acne clears naturally after a few months.

Complementary treatments
Acupressure Pressure on specific acupuncture points may speed healing.

Herbalism Calendula and evening primrose oil have been used successfully to treat acne in older children.

Looks like
Overactive sebaceous glands or milia in newborn baby.

Cradle cap

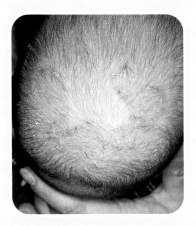

Key signs
Yellowy brown scales on the baby's scalp.

✳✳✳ Very common.

What is it?
A scalp condition that affects babies and occasionally older children. It has nothing to do with poor hygiene and does not mean that the child will develop eczema. Cradle cap that spreads beyond the scalp is one feature of seborrhoeic dermatitis (see opposite).

Symptoms
- Starts under six months.
- Thick scales of skin on the scalp. The scales may be yellowy brown or look like dead skin. The rash does not itch or hurt.
- Red, sore but not itchy skin on the baby's forehead, behind and on the ears or in the nappy area.

What to do
- After the evening bath, rub petroleum jelly or emulsifying ointment gently into the scalp. Baby oil (with or without aloe vera), grapeseed oil, almond oil or pure virgin olive oil will do.
- Warming the oil in your hands makes it easier to massage.
- Protect the cot sheet with a cover.
- In the morning, shampoo the hair and towel it dry. Comb or brush the hair, gently lifting off the scales. Leave them alone if they are still firmly stuck to the scalp.
- Repeat every day until all scales have gone.
- Use a special cradle cap shampoo. Stop if you notice reddening or irritation.

Medical treatment
Rarely needed. Consult a doctor for stubborn cradle cap. A mild hydrocortisone ointment with an antifungal or antibacterial ingredient will treat the condition.

Cradle cap is easy to treat at home, harmless and usually clears within a few days or weeks. It may return, but once the baby's hair has grown you will no longer notice it.

Complementary treatments
Homoeopathy Homoeopathic remedies are tailored to the individual. This is for symptomatic guidance only. Mezereum 12c/30c every 12 hours for three doses if scale is crusty.

Aromatherapy Mix equal quantities of almond and jojoba oil and massage a teaspoonful gently into the scalp once or twice a day. Add one to two drops of tea tree oil to a 50ml (2fl oz) container of baby shampoo, shake well and use a small amount daily until the scalp clears.

Herbalism Massage the scalp with aloe vera lotion or calendula lotion. Check with your health visitor before using herbal remedies on a baby.

Seborrhoeic dermatitis

Key signs
Inflamed, red and flaky rash that does not trouble the baby.

** Common.

What is it?
Seborrhoeic dermatitis is an eczema-type skin rash that appears in the first weeks of life. The most obvious difference from atopic eczema is that the baby is not bothered by the rash because there is no itchiness. The rash is most obvious on the face and the scalp (where you see it as cradle cap) and in the folds of skin.

The cause of seborrhoeic dermatitis in babies isn't well understood, but it is not the same as the seborrhoeic dermatitis that affects adults, which is caused, like dandruff, by an overreaction to the organism Pityrosporum ovale.

Although this condition sounds as if it has a link with the oily sebum glands that produce a milia rash, it actually does not. The rash normally clears in weeks, although it may be more stubborn in the nappy area. Babies with a black skin may be left with lighter skin patches after the rash clears. However, these darken gradually.

Symptoms
- Thick, greasy yellow scales on your baby's head.
- Red patches with a fine yellowish scaling elsewhere, especially on the face, the cheeks, eyebrows and behind the ears.
- Moist, reddened skin in other skinfolds.
- Raw nappy rash that is obvious in the skin creases as well as the skin that touches the nappy.
- The rash is not itchy.

What to do
Consult your doctor to be sure of the diagnosis.

If your baby's scalp is affected, wash his or her hair regularly with a mild cradle cap or medicated shampoo. You can also lightly rub baby or olive oil into the scalp at bedtime. After shampooing the hair in the morning and towelling it dry, gently lift the scales off with a brush or comb. If the flakes resist, leave them alone. Repeat this every day until the scalp clears. Soothe the inflamed patches with a mild emollient such as an aqueous cream.

Medical treatment
If the rash has no secondary infection, your doctor can prescribe a mild hydrocortisone ointment which will clear it in two to three weeks. If there is a secondary infection or it is affected by a spread of the yeast Candida – particularly likely in the nappy area – your doctor may prefer a combination cream with an antifungal or an antibacterial agent.

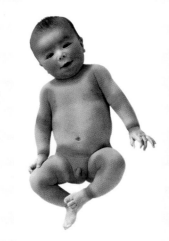

Looks like
Atopic eczema (see pages 68–71).

Heat rash

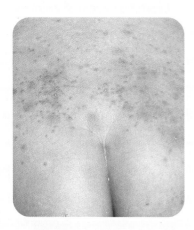

Key signs
Otherwise well baby with pink-red rash in a hot environment.

*** Very common.

Caution
Never leave a baby in a car alone. The temperature inside can rise dangerously fast.

What is it?
Heat rash (prickly heat, miliaria rubra) is the most common rash in young babies, causing a prickly rash of tiny red spots or bumps on parts of the body that easily get hot and sweaty, such as the trunk, nappy area and skin creases.

It develops because the baby's sweat glands are not yet working efficiently and so cannot cool them down. The sweat glands block and leak under the skin, causing a mild inflammation.

Symptoms
- The baby develops a rash of red or pink bumps. Tiny fluid-filled blisters may be seen.
- The rash is on parts of the body that sweat most – in skin creases in the nappy area and the trunk, on the face, neck and shoulders, and under the arms. It's also obvious where clothes are tight fitting.
- Examined with a magnifying glass, a tiny sweat pore is visible at the centre of each red spot.
- A baby with an extensive rash will be restless and irritable.
- The baby's cheeks look hot and pink.

What to do
Heat rash is not serious but, if the rash is still visible hours after the baby has cooled down, contact a doctor.
- Remove one layer of clothing. If the baby remains unusually warm after an hour or so and does not have a fever, give a lukewarm bath. Alternatively, wipe all over, leaving the skin moist. Pat gently dry and replace no more than the

nappy and a cotton vest or T-shirt.
- Offer drinks. If still breastfeeding, give frequent feeds. Once weaned, offer boiled and cooled water or 1:10 diluted juice.
- The temperature in the baby's room should be 16–20°C (60–68°F). Cool with an open window or fan, directed away from the baby.
- Dress in light, low-synthetic clothing.
- Bathe the baby in plain water without additives because inflamed skin is open to further irritation.

Outlook
Blocked sweat glands grow to reach the outer surface of the skin and are replaced by unblocked glands. This takes five to six weeks.

Complementary treatment
Herbalism Always check with your midwife or health visitor before using a herbal remedy for a baby. Calendula lotion or aloe vera is soothing.

Stork marks and mongolian blue spots

Key signs
Pink, red or slate-blue birthmarks.

*** Very common.

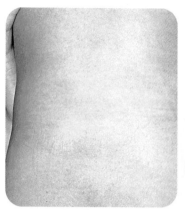

What is it?
These birthmarks in young babies consist of areas of discoloured skin that are visible at birth. Stork marks, also known as angel's kisses, salmon patches or macular stains, appear on the face or the nape of the neck and are pink or red. Mongolian spots appear on the lower back and bottom and look like very large bruises.

Stork marks are caused by collections of tiny dilated blood vessels just beneath the skin. They are more common in white-skinned babies and appear to run in families.

Mongolian spots are caused by large numbers of pigment cells collecting in the deep layers of the skin before birth.

Symptoms
Stork marks
- Dull pink, flat and irregular patches or areas of discoloured skin that get more obvious when the baby cries, strains or is feverish.
- Occur on the nape of the neck, the middle of the forehead, the eyelids or the upper lip. Many babies have more than one patch.

Mongolian blue spots
- Large, irregular and flat, slate-blue patches which can look like bruises.
- Occur chiefly over the lower back and bottom
- Common in Afro-Caribbean, African, Oriental and Hispanic children, but occur occasionally in white children.

What to do
Nothing. They will resolve naturally. If you are concerned, discuss these blemishes with your doctor.

Stork marks on the face will be almost invisible by the baby's first birthday except when he or she strains or cries. Those on the eyelids and lips fade first and forehead marks may still be discernible in toddlers. On the neck they may remain visible until the child is four or even last for life.

Mongolian spots may darken in the first few days of life, but then gradually fade and disappear during childhood. Ensure that they are noted in the baby's child health record.

Outlook
Both types of discoloration are common, completely harmless and disappear eventually without treatment.

Note
The illustration above shows the distribution of stork marks; mongolian blue spots are most common on the lower back and buttocks.

Port wine stain

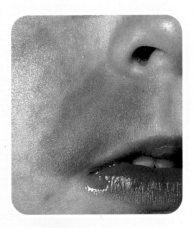

Key signs
Irregularly shaped, pink or
purple birthmark.

* Rare.

Symptoms
- Flat, dark-pink, red or purple
  mark on the skin, most commonly
  on the face although it can occur
  anywhere on the body.
- When the port wine stain is on the
  face, it often occurs near the eye,
  upper or lower jaw. These areas
  are connected to a particular
  nerve – the trigeminal nerve.
- Raised ridges or bumps may
  develop.

What to do
Consult your doctor. The baby will
be referred to a specialist centre for
pulsed dye laser treatment.

Medical treatment
- Laser treatment usually starts
  after the baby is six months old.
  Treatments take place every four
  months. Usually four to six
  treatments are needed,
  depending on the size, depth and
  colour of the stain. Response is
  best if treatment is complete by
  the age of four.
- Laser treatment lightens the stain
  significantly. A superficial stain
  can fade by over 95 per cent.

What is it?
A port wine stain (also called
naevus flammeus) is a birthmark
that consists of a collection of
abnormal capillaries, the body's
tiniest blood vessels. It is flat and
irregular in shape and darkens with
age. It affects three children in
1,000 and is twice as common in
girls as in boys. Untreated, it would
be permanent.

- About one in four children with a
  port wine stain around the eye
  risk developing glaucoma
  (increased pressure in the
  eyeball). Untreated, this can lead
  to blindness. The child requires
  an annual eye check for
  glaucoma.
- Children with port wine stains on
  the upper face and scalp should
  have a magnetic resonance image
  taken to rule out involvement of
  the central nervous system.

What else?
Cosmetic camouflage is available for
special occasions before laser
treatment is complete.

Strawberry mark

What is it?
A type of haemangioma, consisting of a collection of capillaries. Superficial haemangiomas are called strawberry marks. Haemangiomas situated deeper in the skin are called 'deep' or 'cavernous' and appear as a smooth lump, often bluish. Mixed haemangiomas appear as a bluish swelling with a red 'strawberry' surface.

Key signs
Rapidly growing, unsightly but harmless blemish.

** Common.

Caution
Small injuries and rapid growth can cause bleeding. Under pressure, bleeding should stop within 5–10 minutes.

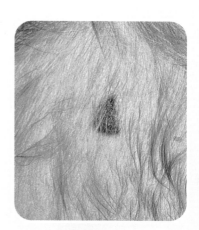

Symptoms
- At birth, invisible or no more than a pink or red mark. A thick-textured lump with a bright red speckled surface then grows.
- A bluish, uneven, smooth lump.
- Commonly on the face and neck, but may occur elsewhere.

What to do
Discuss with a doctor. A strawberry mark that is small, inconspicuous, not in the nappy area and causes the baby no trouble can be allowed to resolve naturally. Increasingly, however, parents choose laser removal. If not:
- Emollient cream keeps the skin supple during growth.
- Barrier cream over a strawberry mark in the nappy area helps prevent ulceration. Ulcers should be bathed twice daily with very dilute potassium permanganate and re-covered with barrier cream. Laser treatment helps any ulcers to heal.

Medical treatments
Laser removal heads the range of medical and surgical treatment options available for marks that are unsightly, troublesome or interfere with vital functions.
- Laser therapy destroys small, flat marks. It also lightens red discoloration to a depth of 1.2mm (1⁄8in). Used together with steroids, it slows the growth rate of large superficial haemangiomas. Unfortunately, laser treatment does not affect a deep haemangioma.
- Steroid treatment slows rapid growth.
- Interferon-alpha slows growth. This treatment is used when vital functions are endangered.
- Gentle freezing at -32°C (-90°), a novel approach, appears to make strawberry marks regress or disappear without scarring.
- Plastic surgery tidies up any scars or loose skin from a large, distorting haemangioma.

What to expect
After rapid growth for the first three months, untreated haemangiomas grow more slowly for a further six months, then gradually shrink and disappear by age five to seven.

Looks like
Stork mark (see page 25). Pressure mark from birth.

Moles, small and large

ABOVE: Congenital moles tend to be larger and darker than moles that appear during childhood.

*** Small moles are very common; large moles are rare.

Note

A baby with a mole over 2.5cm (1in) wide on the scalp or overlying the spine should have a magnetic resonance imaging scan between the ages of one and two to rule out the possibility (estimated at one child in ten) of an associated abnormality.

A baby with a large mole near the eye has an increased risk of glaucoma (increased pressure of the fluid in the eye). He or she will need an annual eye check.

What is it?

Moles (melanocytic naevi) are manufacturing errors in the skin. They consist of clusters of melanocytes, the cells that produce skin's brown pigment melanin. During development, melanocytes travel from the spinal cord down nerves to spread evenly throughout the skin. Moles represent a disruption in that process.

Most moles are flat, harmless and small, measuring just a few millimetres (less than ½in) across, and develop during childhood or later. Much less commonly, babies are born with moles, which can be small, medium sized or, very rarely, so large that they cover an entire limb, body surface, or part of the head and face. These congenital naevi may be flat or raised, smooth or hairy, and tend to be larger and darker than moles which arise during childhood.

Symptoms

- Moles usually appear during childhood and adolescence.
- Most moles are smaller in size than the blunt end of a pencil.
- Moles are darker in dark-skinned children than in fair-skinned types.
- Moles may grow dark hair.
- Moles may be flat or lumpy.
- Large moles may have 'satellite' smaller moles.

What to do

- Nothing at all to the great majority of moles.
- Apply moisturizer if skin becomes dry or itchy.
- Report any changes in shape, colour or proportionate size to a doctor.

- Protect a child with large, congenital or multiple moles against the sun as if they had red hair and blue eyes. Dress them in shading garments. A good sunscreen (factor 25+, with a titanium dioxide base), applied appropriately and regularly, is a last resort for unclothable body parts.

What to expect

Medium-to-large moles usually grow but not as fast as the child. Occasionally, their border also extends in the first years. Parts of the mole may spontaneously darken or lighten. On the face they often have one or two central hairs.

Medical treatment

- Small acquired and congenital moles – the vast majority – are left alone.
- Unsightly moles can be removed by excision for cosmetic reasons. A small scar remains, however.

Key signs

Most moles develop during childhood and are small, harmless and usually flat. Much more rarely, babies are born with congenital moles that are variable in size and appearance. The great majority are harmless, although malignant changes can arise, albeit rarely, especially in very large congenital moles.

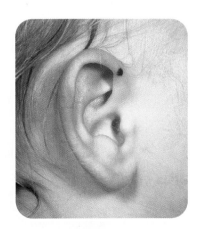

- Any mole that changes in size, shape or colour or becomes inflamed or irritated should be examined for malignant changes. Removal usually involves a small operation under a local anaesthetic. Any scar should be inconspicuous.
- Removing a large congenital mole involves lifting off the full skin thickness or part of it. Removing part of the skin's thickness allows new skin to grow and cover any remaining discoloration. It is usually carried out by a process called dermabrasion (shaving) or using a carbon dioxide laser. The procedure appears most successful in children under two, particularly babies. However, results are unpredictable and variable.

- Larger, lumpier and hairier moles usually need removal of the full skin thickness. Full thickness removal should start and ideally be finished by the age of four. The skin is then replaced by: grafting (removing skin from another part of the body); rotation flaps (flaps of skin that are partly lifted off adjacent areas); or tissue expansion (skin 'grown' by implanting a temporary balloon which forces it to grow).
- For larger moles, both full and partial thickness removal are often performed.

What else?

Black children are quite frequently born with large, flat, pale brown moles (café-au-lait spots) that are harmless.

Looks like

Freckles, although freckles fade in winter.

Nappy rash

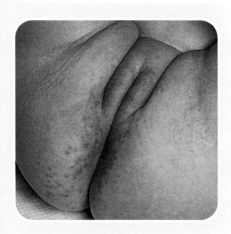

ABOVE: **Babies with a sensitive skin are more prone to nappy rash.**

Looks like
Seborrhoeic dermatitis
(see page 23)
Psoriasis (see pages 82–83),
although this is very rare in
babies.

What is it?
Usually a reaction to urine and faeces, nappy rash is an irritant dermatitis, caused by sealing the bottom in a urine-soaked environment, which makes the skin vulnerable to irritation. Breakdown products of urine and faeces include ammonia, which burns the skin.

Simple nappy rash is commonly complicated by thrush (see pages 86–87).

Symptoms
- Red patches or spots on the skin in contact with the nappy. They may look shiny and glazed.
- A rash of bright red pimples spreading from the anus.
- Red patches spreading beyond the nappy area to the chest and back.

What to do
- Leave the baby nappy free whenever possible.
- Change nappies often, at your bedtime and at night feeds.
- At each nappy change gently but thoroughly wash all urine and faeces off the bottom. Instead of astringent wipes, use warm tap water with aqueous cream or bath oil as a cleanser. If you want to use wipes, choose ones that are hypoallergenic, pH balanced and alcohol free and use gently. Pat thoroughly dry. Moisturize the skin with aqueous cream, zinc and castor oil, or a barrier cream. Spray-on creams penetrate the skin creases.
- Fit an oversize nappy. If using cloth nappies, insert a nappy liner and use covers made of natural fibres instead of plastic pants.
- When dressing the baby, avoid clothes that hug the groin. When transporting them avoid tight straps or slings.
- Nappy types don't cause nappy rash, but babies in disposables get it less often. Rinse washing powder thoroughly out of cloth nappies and use a non-biological washing powder or one for sensitive skins.
- Be vigilant while your baby has a cold or diarrhoea, or is teething, being weaned or on antibiotics.

Key signs
Instantly recognizable sore red patches in nappy area.

✱✱✱ Mild nappy rash is extremely common; a severe rash is rare.

Note
Healing skin may appear pale in a dark-skinned baby. It gradually darkens.

Medical treatments
Rarely necessary. A pharmacist can supply an antifungal cream for thrush or a doctor can prescribe it. Apply it for at least a week after the rash has resolved. A mild steroid cream speeds healing, but apply it for no more than one week. Using plastic pants intensifies absorption of steroid and should be avoided.

Outlook
Once your baby is out of nappies, nappy rash ends.

Complementary treatments
Herbalism Apply calendula (antiseptic) ointment; apricot kernel oil, evening primrose oil or avocado oil; or aloe vera gel (soothing). Or bathe in a lotion made up from 10 drops of Calendula mother tincture to half a cup of sterilized water. Check with your health visitor before using herbal products on a baby with nappy rash.

Homoeopathy Borax 30c helps if the baby is prone to thrush; Calc Carb 30c when the rash itches and smarts, Graphites 30c if the skin is rough and easily chafed, Hepar Sulph 30c if the skin is inflamed and itching, and Sulphur 30c for itchy, scaly red rash. Repeat the dose three times, every three to four hours. Apply Urtica Urens cream.
Aromatherapy Clean your baby's bottom with jojoba oil. To a 50g (2oz) pot of fragrance-free nappy rash cream, add two drops lavender oil and two drops camomile. Apply a fine layer no more than twice a day. Add one drop of lavender or camomile oil to a tablespoon of milk and stir it in your baby's bath.

Rashes with fever

Diagnosis

A rash with a fever (a temperature over 38°C/100°F) is usually a sign that your child has caught an infection. The rash and fever usually appear at roughly the same time, though the fever often comes first and in some infections, such as roseola, the rash only emerges as the fever subsides. When trying to find the cause of the rash, undress your child completely or you will miss important clues. Most hard-to-identify rash infections are caused by a virus such as coxsackie or echo virus and clear up quickly without problems. As many rashes with fever are infectious, it's important to consult a doctor for diagnosis.

Contagious rashes spread by direct contact, while infectious illnesses usually spread by droplet infection, when an affected child breathes out infected droplets, and another person inhales them. Most rashes with fever spread by droplet infection, but the rashes that cause blisters (chickenpox and hand, foot and mouth disease) also spread by direct contact.

It would be helpful to give a doctor or nurse the answers to these questions.

- How long has your child had the rash?

- Is it moving or changing?

- Did the fever start first?

- Is your child very unwell or is your child getting worse?

- Is it itchy, hot or uncomfortable?

- Has anyone else with whom your child mixes recently had a similar rash?

- What medicines have you given your child?

- What creams or lotions have you used for the rash?

- Have you been abroad recently?

For a rash that doesn't disappear when you press it under a clear glass, see
Meningitis and septicaemia
Purpura

For a fine, pink or red, blotchy rash, see
Measles
Kawasaki disease
Roseola
Rubella
Scarlet fever
Viral rash

For a red rash over the cheeks, see
Slapped cheek disease

For a localized rash, see
Cellulitis
Lyme disease

For a rash of blisters, see
Chickenpox
Hand, foot and mouth disease

Lyme disease

Key signs
Expanding flat red rash after a tick bite, usually in woodlands.

* Uncommon.

Caution
Infection of the nervous system can cause serious complications.
Can cause pain and arthritis. Rarely, can lead to heart disorders.

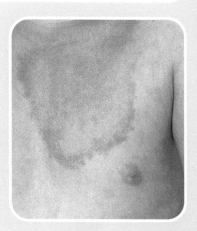

What is it?
Lyme disease is an infection carried by ticks infected with the Borrelia burgdorferi bacterium. Although it occasionally causes a mild flu-like illness, the first sign is usually a typical circular red rash around the bite.

Symptoms
- A very large, circular red rash – like a stone thrown into a pond – expanding from a tick bite. As the rash spreads, the centre clears.
- A rash of smaller circular red patches.
- General malaise, including fever, tiredness, headache, and joint and muscle pains.
- Swollen glands, especially in the neck.

What to do
Lyme disease cannot be treated at home, so take the child promptly to a doctor. Tell him or her of any recent visits to the countryside, particularly to woodland. The following are the steps to take to protect yourself and your family:
- Cover up when walking in grass or woodlands. Wear long trousers tucked into socks and long-sleeved tops.
- Spray or rub on insect repellent.
- Check children regularly for ticks. Remove gently but firmly, without squeezing, but ensuring that all mouth parts are removed. Cover the tick in petroleum jelly for 15 minutes first (thus suffocating it) for easier removal.
- A Lyme disease vaccine is licensed in the USA but not for children.

Medical treatment
- The doctor may take a blood sample to help to confirm the diagnosis.
- They will prescribe a three- to four-week course of antibiotics.
- Ibuprofen relieves pain.
- If not treated promptly, Lyme disease may need intravenous antibiotic therapy.

Note
- Unfed ticks are so tiny that it is easy to miss them. After a meal an adult tick is the size of a coffee bean.
- Ticks prefer damp woodlands and mild weather. Their numbers drop after hot, dry weather and in winter.
- Many ticks do not carry Lyme disease.
- People with Lyme disease are not infectious.

Incubation
Typically 7–14 days, can be 3–30.

Immunity
None.

How it is spread
Ticks transmit the Borrelia bacterium when they bite and suck blood.

Meningitis and septicaemia

What is it?
Meningitis is an inflammation of the lining of the brain. Septicaemia is an infection in the bloodstream. Both infections frequently develop together. They can be caused by a variety of viruses or bacteria.

Viral meningitis is generally less serious; bacterial meningitis and septicaemia (which includes that caused by Haemophilus influenzae b – Hib) develop swiftly and need urgent antibiotic treatment. The two main types of bacterial infection are:
- Meningococcal: of the two most common strains, group B infection is now more common since the introduction of the vaccine against group C infection.
- Pneumococcal, still common in UK: children under two in the USA are immunized against pneumococcal infection.

How it is spread
By droplets on the breath, infectious agents reach the lining of the back of the nose and throat, and pass into the bloodstream.
- The organisms that cause bacterial meningitis do not live for long outside the body so they are not passed on in public places such as buses, swimming pools or parks.
- Meningitis occurs all year round with peaks in winter.

What causes it?
Infectious agents inflame the meninges, the tough, protective membranes that cover the brain inside the skull, causing meningitis. In an apparently increasing number of children the bacteria multiply in the blood, causing septicaemia. This can develop very fast, in a few hours, and is especially serious. Meningococcal bacteria are most likely to cause this form of blood poisoning.

Symptoms
At first it looks like a bad cold or flu. It is difficult to spot early in babies and young children.

Babies and children show some of these signs. They may not display them all and the signs may develop in any order:
- Pin-prick rash, marks or purple bruises that don't go white, even for a few seconds, when pressed (under a glass).
- Fever/vomiting between any feeds.
- Cold hands and feet.
- Rapid/difficult breathing.
- Stomach/joint/muscle pain.
- Too sleepy to wake up, staring.
- Severe headache.
- Dislikes light.

Babies may also have:
- A tense or bulging fontanelle (soft spot on top of head).
- Blotchy skin, getting paler or turning blue.
- An irritable, shrill, moaning cry when handled.
- A stiff, jerky body or a floppy body.

They may also refuse feeds.

There is frequently no rash in pneumococcal meningitis and septicaemia.

What to do
- Call your doctor or emergency medical helpline urgently and describe the symptoms. Follow their instructions. You may be asked to take the child immediately to hospital or to wait until the doctor arrives. If the doctor suspects meningitis or meningococcal septicaemia, the child will be given an immediate injection of penicillin, or an alternative antibiotic if the child is allergic to penicillin. The

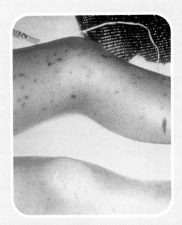

Key signs
Non-blanching rash in clearly unwell child.

* Rare.

Incubation
Two to seven days for meningococcal disease, and possibly one to three days for pneumococcal disease.

Immunity
Babies are routinely offered immunization against the two kinds of bacteria formerly responsible for many cases of meningitis – Hib infection and group C meningococcal infection.

A pneumococcal vaccine is now available for babies with certain health conditions. Vaccine trials against group B meningococcal disease have taken place and the prospect of a vaccine is hopeful.

doctor will usually take a swab from the nose and throat to identify the infection.
- Once the diagnosis is confirmed, all friends, family and school must be informed.
- Local health authorities will trace close contacts of the child and offer everyone in the household contact a course of protective antibiotics.

Medical treatment
The child is given antibiotics and sometimes steroids to reduce inflammation and pressure inside the skull. Drugs to stop convulsions, pain relief and fluids may also be given. To identify the infective agent, the child has blood tests and almost certainly a lumbar puncture, in which a tiny quantity of the fluid round the spine is drawn off from a space in the backbone between the vertebrae. Children with meningitis or septicaemia frequently need intensive care, with their breathing and heart mechanically supported.

Outlook
Advances in treatment have recently led to a tenfold fall in the numbers of even the most severely affected children dying. Today more than three-quarters of children recover completely from bacterial meningitis, although some are left with permanent handicaps such as deafness and brain damage. Many children show signs of damage to their nervous system, which usually clears within a month. Hearing may be temporarily affected, so children can expect a hearing check after recovery. Short-term memory may be temporarily lost and behavioural difficulties are common but usually fade within 6–12 months.

Looks like
Viral infections.
Purpura (see page 38).

Purpura

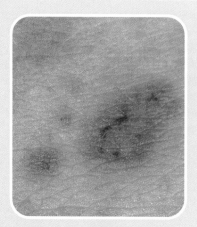

Key signs
Non-blanching spots in a child who may have had a viral or other infection.

* Rare.

Looks like
Meningococcal septicaemia (see pages 36–37).

Symptoms
- Dark-red irregular spots, ranging from a pinhead to 2cm (1in) across.
- The spots do not fade when pressed with a glass or a finger.
- Centre of each spot may be raised.
- Most spots on the legs and bottom.
- The child may recently have had a viral infection.
- Occasionally, painful joints, stomach ache, rust-coloured urine.

Purpura may be one of a cluster of symptoms, pointing to a specific diagnosis. Henoch–Schönlein purpura causes painful, occasionally swollen joints, abdominal pain and kidney inflammation, as well as the characteristic non-fading rash, usually in response to a viral infection. It may recur after subsequent infections.

Thrombocytopenic purpura is a rare side effect of MMR immunization and shows as a rash of small, bruise-like spots appearing within six weeks of being vaccinated (see page 85).

What is it?
Purpura is a rash caused by blood leaking out of the capillaries, the tiniest blood vessels. It has a number of different causes, all involving the blood's ability to clot or a breakdown in the walls of the capillaries. Infection, an allergic reaction or a drug reaction leading to an inflammation of the blood vessels are common causes. Meningococcal septicaemia is a serious cause.

What to do
Contact a doctor or medical service immediately. Although the cause of purpura is usually not serious, it is important for an acute infection such as meningococcal septicaemia or meningitis to be ruled out.

Medical treatment
- No specific treatment is needed for the rash.
- If the kidneys are involved, the child may need treatment.
- The cause of the infection will be investigated and treated.

Outlook
- The rash will fade in one to three weeks.
- The child usually recovers fully.
- Occasionally children get repeat attacks of purpura following infections.

Viral rash

What is it?
Many viruses that children meet frequently cause a mild cold or flu-like illness and a rash. The rash is rarely distinctive, but usually has flat, red spots, sometimes separate, sometimes joined up as pink-red blotches. Echo and Coxsackie viruses are most commonly involved.

Many other transient rashes (such as food and medicine reactions) are passed off as viral rashes.

Symptoms
- Rash of flat red spots that sometimes join up to form reddish blotches.
- Rash rarely itches.
- On pressure with a glass, rash usually fades.
- Possibly slight fever and malaise.

What to do
- Give infant paracetamol or ibuprofen for any fever or discomfort.
- Consult doctor if the child is taking antibiotics. Viral rashes look very similar to rashes caused by an allergic reaction to antibiotics. An allergic rash is more likely to itch.

Key signs
Unidentified, often fleeting rash in a child who is no more than mildly unwell.

*** Extremely common.

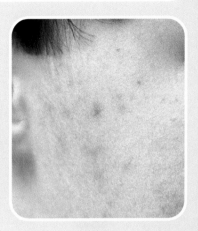

Looks like
Drug or food reactions and allergies.

Roseola

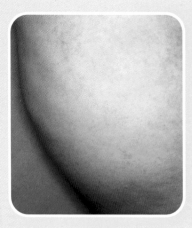

Key signs
Widespread splotchy pink rash spreads as high fever subsides.

*** Common.

Incubation
Unknown, but probably 5–15 days.

Caution
Very high fever can bring on febrile convulsions.

Looks like
Measles (see page 42).
Rubella (see opposite).

How it is spread
Caused by an organism in the herpes family – human herpes virus 6.

Immunity
By age one, three-quarters of babies have natural immunity.

Symptoms
- An abrupt fever. A very sharp rise puts the infant at risk of a febrile convulsion.
- Grizzly behaviour, sore throat, going off feeds.
- Slightly swollen neck glands.
- As the fever drops after three to five days, a rash of splotchy rose spots appears over the chest, abdomen and back before spreading to the arms and neck. On the thighs and bottom, each spot may be surrounded by a fine halo. The rash rarely lasts more than two days.

What to do
Contact your doctor or emergency medical service to discuss the symptoms. It is important to rule out rubella and measles as causes of the rash.
- Reduce fever by giving infant paracetamol or ibuprofen and extra clear fluids.
- Cool by tepid sponging. Undress to nappy/underwear, lay child on a towel and, using a basin of warm water and two moist facecloths, wipe face, arms,

What is it?
Also known as sixth disease or exanthem subitum ('sudden rash'), it is a mild infection caused by a herpes virus. Roseola is very common among babies and young children, especially between six months and two years.

chest, back and legs. Pat gently dry or allow to dry naturally. The temperature should start to fall within 5–15 minutes. Sit a toddler in a bath with a few inches of warm water, sponge for 10–20 minutes, pat dry and dress lightly.
- Without paracetamol the temperature usually climbs back to pre-sponging levels within half an hour.
- Offer frequent cool drinks. Offer a breastfed baby a feed on demand, or every hour.
- Appetite loss for a day or two is not important.

Outlook
Complete recovery within two to three days.

Complementary treatment
Herbalism Herbal preparations containing Echinacea are reputed to stimulate the immune system, whereas herbal teas containing mint or ginger may reduce fever and boost fluid intake. Consult a doctor before giving a child with roseola herbal preparations.

Rubella

Key signs
Tiny, separate pink or red spots over face, joining up as rash spreads over body.

* Rare.

Incubation
14–21 days.

Caution
Avoid contact with pregnant women.

What is it?
Rubella (German measles) is a mild viral infection producing a rash so fleeting that it often vanishes before a doctor can confirm it. A trivial infection were it not for the effects on the unborn baby.

Symptoms
- Non-specific at first – cough, sore eyes, runny nose, reluctance to feed.
- Tiny, pinkish-red, flat spots spread within hours from behind ears and forehead to face and body.
- As rash spreads, the temperature may rise to 38°C (100.4°F). Any fever drops when the rash fades, within two days.
- Swollen glands at the back of the neck and beneath the ears.

What to do
For a definite diagnosis, make a doctor's appointment for blood or saliva to be taken for analysis.
- Rubella is infectious from about one week before the rash appears until four days after. Keep the child off school/nursery until five days after the rash emerges.
- Recently immunized children are not infectious.
- Relieve discomfort from fever.
- Keep the child away from women who might be pregnant until four days after the rash has faded.
- Potentially devastating effects on the unborn baby in the first 16 weeks of pregnancy. Congenital rubella syndrome (i.e. rubella contracted in the womb in the early months of pregnancy) presents as any combination of eye problems, deafness, heart defects, slow growth and learning disability. If contracted in the first 8–10 weeks, as many as 90 per cent of such babies are affected. By 16 weeks only 10–20 per cent are affected. After 16 weeks, damage to the unborn baby is rare.

Complementary treatments
Homoeopathy One tablet/two to three drops of Rubella 30c Nosode, with second dose after 24 hours if symptoms are severe or child is failing to recover. For other remedies, see measles (page 42).
Herbalism Only give herbal remedies to your child with your doctor's knowledge. Mint tea is said to be soothing and both goldenseal and Echinacea are reputed to boost the immune system. However, goldenseal should not be given to under-twos.

Looks like
Many other childhood infections, viral rashes or drug rashes.

How it is spread
By droplets of the rubella virus on the breath.

Immunity
A highly effective (95 per cent take rate) live vaccine given as part of MMR (mumps/measles/rubella) programme.

Measles

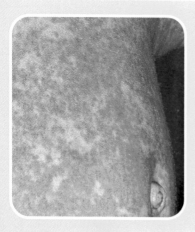

Key signs
Widespread, red rash emerges in child with high fever for three or more days. White spots inside cheeks.

* Normally rare.

Incubation
9–11 days.

Looks like
Rubella (see page 41).
Scarlet fever (see opposite).
Roseola (see page 40).
Kawasaki disease (see page 47) (rare).

How it is spread
Droplet spread and direct contact with nasal secretions.

Infectious?
Four days before appearance of rash to four days after.

Symptoms
Symptoms develop in the following order:
- Irritable and tired, with fever that can reach 40°C (105°F).
- Appetite loss, runny nose and dry hacking cough.
- Sore red eyes and sensitivity to light.
- White spots inside cheeks.
- Rash of red spots, usually first on the forehead, spreading down the body. Spots can join up to form large red-brown blotches.
- On black skin no redness shows. Instead the surface is rough, like sandpaper.
- As rash spreads, the fever drops.
- Also stomach ache, diarrhoea, vomiting and swollen glands.

What to do
Contact a doctor to check diagnosis.
- Give infant paracetamol or ibuprofen and clear drinks for fever.
- Make your child comfortable.
- Keep child away from anyone who has not been immunized and off nursery or school for five days from emergence of rash.

What is it?
Highly infectious viral disease with a whole-body rash of small red spots that join up to form blotches.

- Stay alert for complications – rising fever, worsening cough, failure to improve after three to four days.
- Complications are common: one child in 15 develops bronchitis, ear infections or pneumonia. Rare, more serious complications include encephalitis and SSPE (subacute sclerosing panencephalomyelitis), a slowly advancing brain infection that can cause permanent brain damage.

Medical treatment
Usually none. Diagnosis should be confirmed by saliva test. Antibiotics will be needed for secondary complications.

Outlook
After around three days the child starts to feel better.

Immunity
Inherited immunity fades by eight months. Immunity after infection is usually life-long.

Scarlet fever

Key signs
Blush-like rash with red spots typically sparing skin round the mouth.

** Fairly common.

Incubation
Two to four (rarely seven) days.

Caution
Very rarely causes serious complications.

What is it?
Scarlet fever (scarlatina) is a bacterial infection caused by a streptococcus. Scarlet fever used to be serious but most cases today are mild, perhaps because the bacterium has become less virulent. It is rare in babies under 12 months and most common in primary school-age children.

Symptoms
- Sore throat.
- Fever.
- Loses interest in food. May vomit.
- After one to three days, rash of pinhead red spots appears on the neck, back or chest. The rash spreads fast over the body and face and usually lasts two to three days, but occasionally disappears sooner.
- As the rash fades, any sore throat settles and the temperature drops.
- The skin now has a rough sandpaper feel.
- A week after the rash appears, the skin may peel in flakes from the fingers and toes, or in a fine powder from the body.
- The tongue may have a white coating with red spots. After a day or two, the coating reveals a strawberry-red tongue.
- Sometimes complications occur: the most common are ear infections, kidney disease and rheumatic fever developing two to three weeks after the rash emerges.

What to do
- Give infant paracetamol or ibuprofen for fever.
- Encourage child to drink non-acidic juices or bland milky drinks. Try drinking yoghurt, melted ice cream or a milk shake with a wide straw.
- To relieve the discomfort of a high temperature, tepid sponge.
- Consult a doctor.

Medical treatment
A throat swab confirms the diagnosis. Some doctors allow a mild case of scarlet fever to take its natural course. Most prescribe antibiotics (penicillin unless allergic) for a child who is clearly unwell and to prevent complications. The child remains infectious until a day after the fever subsides or 24 hours after starting a course of antibiotics.

Outlook
Once the child has been on antibiotics for 48 hours he or she usually starts to feel better. With treatment, scarlet fever usually lasts about a week.

Looks like
Kawasaki disease (see page 47).
Measles (see opposite).

How it is spread
By droplet infection.
- Direct contact with infected items, such as tissues.
- Often spread by people who are not symptomatic.

Immunity
Usually life-long.

Hand, foot & mouth disease

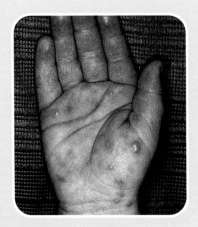

Key signs
Small blisters on palms, soles and in mouth in unwell child.

** Fairly common.

Incubation
Three to five days.

Caution
On very rare occasions can be serious for very young infants.

What is it?
Mild viral illness caused by highly infectious Coxsackie virus; small blisters appear on the hands and feet and inside the mouth.

It has no connection with the foot and mouth disease that affects sheep and other animals.

Common in young children, especially in day care, nursery or playgroup. Outbreaks most common in summer and mild weather.

Symptoms
- Sore throat and reluctance to eat.
- Fever and general malaise.
- Tiny blisters appear inside the cheeks, on the gums and sides of the tongue. They develop into shallow grey ulcers on a red base. These blisters usually take 7–10 days to heal.
- Small, clear and sometimes itchy blisters encircled with red appear on the palms and soles. They sometimes show on the backs of the hands, in nail folds and under the arms. A baby's nappy area may, rarely, be affected.
- Doctors suspect that many people show no symptoms.

What to do
Treat at home but consult a doctor if uncertain of the diagnosis.
- Dab calamine on blisters to relieve itching.
- Avoid acidic fruit juices while the mouth is sore.
- Give children's paracetamol or ibuprofen for fever and encourage the child to drink.
- The child remains infectious for up to seven days. Keep child away from nursery, school or playgroup until the crusts that develop from the hand and foot blisters have dropped off or the fluid in the blisters has been reabsorbed. He or she is most infectious now and quite likely to pass the virus on.
- Limit the spread of the virus by washing toys and hands frequently. Be meticulous with nappy hygiene because virus lingers in the faeces for several weeks after recovery.
- Leave the nappy off when possible if this area is affected.

Looks like
Chickenpox (see page 48).
Aphthous ulcers (in mouth).

How it is spread
By direct contact with rash or in droplets on the breath.
- Possibly from faeces.
- It is not caught from family pets or any other animals.

Immunity
Imparted through infection.
Infants born with no immunity.

Slapped cheek disease

Key signs
Hot red flush over cheeks, spreading as lacy red rash over body, arms and legs.

*** Very common.

Incubation
13–18 days.

Cautions
Risky to pregnant women. May cause miscarriage.

What is it?
A mild viral infection caused by the not-very-infectious human parvovirus B19, which gives a bright red rash on the cheeks and rubella-like symptoms. Also known as fifth disease or erythema infectiosum.

Common among primary school children; a quarter of people who catch it have no symptoms.

Symptoms
- The child may be unwell for one to two days with a slight fever. This phase is more obvious in adults and antedates rash by three to four days.
- A rash of pink-red spots starts on the cheeks, which look raw and feel hot to the touch. The rash looks very like rubella. It often spreads to the back, abdomen and legs, and may come and go for up to three weeks. The rash sometimes fades from the centre, giving the skin a blotchy or lacy appearance.

epidemics among children. A child who is well need not miss school, because children are no longer infectious once the rash has appeared.
- Contact anyone who might be pregnant and has been in contact with your child.

Outlook
- Full recovery, although rash may last as long as six weeks.
- For months after recovery, children may develop bright red cheeks again in sunlight, when overheated or excited.

What to do
Slapped cheek disease is normally so mild in children that it resolves without treatment.
- If the child is unwell, keep him or her at home.
- Give infant paracetamol or ibuprofen for fever.
- Cool burning cheeks with a refrigerated (not frozen) icepack or facecloth.
- Inform the child's nursery or school because slapped cheek disease can occur in mini-

Note
Slapped cheek disease can trigger crisis in people with blood disorders such as sickle-cell disease or thalassaemia.

Looks like
Rubella (see page 41).

How it is spread
By droplets on the breath.

Infectious?
For a week before rash emerges. No longer infectious once rash appears.

Immunity
Thought to be life-long; 60 per cent of adults are immune.

Cellulitis

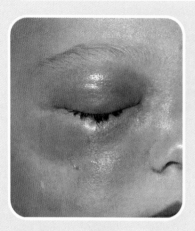

Key signs
Hot, red, tender and
swollen skin, usually
affecting an arm or leg,
or the face.

✱ **Rare in babies and
children.**

Looks like
Slapped cheek disease (on the
face) (see page 45).

Symptoms
- Hot, red, tender and swollen skin,
  usually covering a well-defined
  area.
- Swelling feels hard to the touch.
- Can affect any part of the body
  but most common on a limb, the
  face and around the eyes.
  Swelling around the eye may be
  so great that the child cannot
  open it. Typically, cellulitis on the
  face stretches across the bridge
  of the nose to both cheeks.
- Possibly fever. The child may be
  generally unwell.
- Dark-red spots may occur in
  swollen tissue.
- Extremely swollen skin may
  blister.

What is it?
Spreading bacterial infection of the
deep, lower layers of the skin and
the tissues beneath. Usually caused
by a streptococcus. Repeated
attacks in the same area may be
caused by poor or obstructed lymph
drainage. Cellulitis affecting the
face is sometimes called
erysipelas.

What to do
- Contact a doctor.
- Encourage the child to rest. Raise
  an affected arm or leg. Cool it
  with cloths wrung out in cold
  water or, if the child is not
  feverish, by directing a cold fan
  at it.
- Give children's paracetamol or
  ibuprofen to relieve fever and
  discomfort.

Medical treatment
The doctor will prescribe a course of
antibiotics, usually for 10–14 days
but as long as necessary to clear the
infection.

Outlook
Normally resolves completely
following antibiotic treatment.
The child will feel much better in
a day or two but the swelling may
take a few weeks to subside. As it
heals, the skin may peel but no
scarring is left.

Kawasaki disease

Key signs
Very unwell child, red rash, swollen extremities and sore, cracked mouth.

∗ **Rare.**

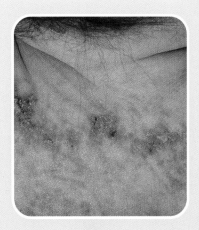

What is it?
A severe illness chiefly affecting children under five, Kawasaki disease (mucocutaneous lymph node syndrome) is presumed to be an infection.

No virus or bacterium has been identified and it does not appear to pass from person to person.

Symptoms
The disease starts with a high fever and downright misery. Other symptoms develop, though not necessarily at the same time and not all children have them all.

At least five of the six symptoms are needed for diagnosis:
- Fluctuating high fever lasting five days or more.
- Red rash, sometimes angriest in the nappy area.
- Red, bloodshot eyes usually with no watering.
- Palms of the hands and soles of the feet turn red and swollen.
- Red, swollen, dry and cracked lips; 'strawberry-like' tongue; red inside the mouth.
- Of children affected, 50–75 per cent get tender swollen glands in the neck.

What to do
Contact a doctor at the first suspicion. This is an uncommon disease that is difficult to diagnose and has no definitive test so the doctor may take a few days to reach a decision.

Medical treatment
In hospital the child is made comfortable and given fluids if dehydrated. If Kawasaki disease is confirmed the child receives gamma-globulin (a preparation of antibodies) and aspirin.

Outlook
Once treatment is under way, the child should start feeling better within 24–48 hours. After the serious phase of the illness (which usually lasts about 10 days), the child will usually be well enough to go home. In the second or third week, the skin may peel. There may be joint pains. Full recovery may take 10–12 weeks.

During the high fever, the inflammation can affect the lining and muscle of the heart. In the first four weeks aneurysms (ballooning) can develop in the coronary arteries. In a small number of children, a blood clot may form in these areas.

Most children get over Kawasaki disease without lasting harm. With medical treatment most artery abnormalities eventually recover.

Looks like
Viral infection.
Measles (see page 42).
Scarlet fever (see page 43).

What else?
- Sixteen years' follow-up shows that most children recover with no further problems.
- The child should not have MMR vaccine within three months of receiving gamma-globulin or of having Kawasaki disease.

Chickenpox

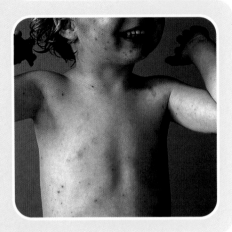

ABOVE: **A child with chickenpox is frequently not unwell.**

How it is spread

By direct contact with the fluid in the blisters or by droplets on the breath.

- A person with chickenpox is infectious from a day or so before the first spots appear. Infectivity (i.e. the ability to infect others) is highest as the first crop of spots breaks and lasts for the first five spotty days.

What is it?

An infection caused by varicella-zoster virus. Usually mild, chickenpox can occasionally lead to serious complications, including pneumonia, fits and encephalitis (inflammation of the brain).

Symptoms

- Red or pink pimples appear on the scalp, face or back, spreading to the arms and legs.
- Within hours they develop into small fluid-filled blisters. One to two spots or whole-body rash.
- Blisters recede or, usually, form intensely itchy yellow crust after three to four days.
- Slight fever, appetite loss and possibly sore throat
- Crops of spots appear for up to five days.
- Symptoms in older children are frequently more severe.

What to do

Treat the child yourself if you are confident of the diagnosis, and he or she usually throws off coughs and colds easily.

- Give paracetamol or ibuprofen and clear drinks for a raised temperature.
- Inform the child's school and other contacts, especially pregnant women.
- To relieve itching, dab aqueous calamine cream on to the spots with cotton wool. Give the child

his or her own supply to press, pat or pinch on the spots.
- Give a daily cool/tepid bath with a handful of bicarbonate of soda dissolved in it.
- Keep the child cool. Dress in loose clothes.
- Give an antihistamine medicine at bedtime to relieve itching and encourage sleep.
- Trim nails to limit damage by scratching. Put cotton mitts or socks on a baby.
- Five days after the first spots appear the child can return to nursery, day care or school.

Medical treatment

Consult a doctor if the child is clearly unwell, if the spots become red and infected, the temperature rises or a cough develops. The doctor can prescribe the antiviral medicine aciclovir for older children or adults with a severe attack.

Outlook

After an attack of chickenpox, the virus can lie in a resting state in nerve cells, and may develop into shingles (see page 90) on

Key signs
Itchy blisters on red bases, anywhere on face or body, in unwell child.

*** Very common.

Incubation
7–21 days.

Caution
Always serious in a young baby who inherited no antibodies from their mother. However, most babies are born with six months' worth of protective antibodies.

Serious in children with leukaemia or children taking immunosuppressive medication.

Immunity
One attack normally gives life-long immunity.

Vaccine is available in the USA. In the UK, vaccine is available for high-risk children (such as children on immunosuppressive treatment).

reactivation, sometimes many years later.

Complementary treatments
Herbalism Add burdock or sarsaparilla to the bath or soak a facecloth in an infusion of either herb. Camomile (as cream or tea), yarrow and/or lavender soothes. Ginger can calm restlessness and aloe vera gel soothes itchy spots.
Homoeopathy As a preventive, give Rhus Tox 30c from time of contact. If child catches chickenpox, continue. Give Varicella 30c for severe attack or complications. Give remedies every three to four hours for two to three days.

Pregnant women
Pregnant women should avoid close contact with anyone with chickenpox or shingles. There is a small but real chance that the infection might affect the unborn baby if the mother is not already immune. Most women are immune even if they have no memory of having chickenpox as a child. Your doctor can check your immune status with a blood sample.

Should a pregnant woman turn out not to be immune, she can be given antibodies in a form known as VZIG (varicella-zoster immunoglobulin). So long as VZIG is given soon after contact it will make the chickenpox less severe and may reduce the risk of the baby catching it. The vast majority of babies are not affected if their mother catches chickenpox while pregnant, but a tiny number (less than one per cent in the first 12 weeks and around two per cent in weeks 13 to 20) may develop quite severe chickenpox-related defects. Babies who catch chickenpox around delivery may be especially severely affected and may themselves be given VZIG.

Children on oral steroids in contact with chickenpox should be advised whether VZIG will help prevent a severe attack.

Chickenpox and shingles
Someone with shingles can very occasionally give a child chickenpox. The opposite – that a child with chickenpox activates shingles in someone else – doesn't happen.

Looks like
Impetigo (see page 60) or insect bites (see page 88), which is quite unusual. Hand, foot and mouth disease (see page 44).

Rashes spread by skin contact

Diagnosis

Skin conditions carry a stigma even among very young children. They act as a visible difference and serve as a way for children to cruelly draw social boundaries between themselves and non-friends. The stigma is that much worse when the skin condition is transmitted by direct contact, however unlikely that is. All the conditions in this brief section can be caught from other children or adults. While most of them are not a reason for a child to stay off school, at least once treatment has started (see School rules, page 9), all of them can make the child a focus of teasing or bullying. Open, sensitive discussion within a class can deflect latent bullying.

Open discussion also makes contact tracing easier and this is an important step towards controlling contagious infections and infestations.

For rashes that make the child scratch, especially at night, see
Scabies

For a rash that makes the child scratch his or her hair, see
Headlice
Ringworm

For a rash of itchy red circles, see
Ringworm

For a crop of small wart-like lumps anywhere on the body, see
Molluscum

For separate flesh-coloured or whitish circular lumps, see
Verrucas
Warts

For sores on the face, see
Impetigo
Cold sores

Ringworm

What is it?

Ringworm (tinea) is a fungal infection often caught from family pets, especially kittens and puppies. It is not caused by a worm. Microscopic spores of the ringworm fungus brush off the animal's fur onto the child's skin, lodging in a tiny cut, graze or patch of eczema.

Ringworm is not serious, but it is unsightly and embarrassing. Scalp ringworm (tinea capitis) needs prompt treatment to avoid bald patches developing.

Key signs

Itchy, red inflamed circles that spread outwards, leaving pale skin in the centre. On the head, can look like itchy dandruff.

** Common.

Incubation

Probably two to four weeks.

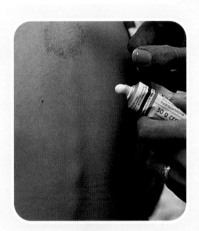

Symptoms

- On the body: round/oval red, itchy and sometimes scaly patches with centres of healed skin. Most common on the face; also on body, arms and legs.
- On the head: circles of scaly skin that become inflamed and swollen. As the centre heals, hairs snap off, leaving stubble and a moth-eaten appearance.

What to do

If you are confident with the diagnosis, ringworm on the body can usually be treated at home. Otherwise, consult a doctor. Ringworm on the scalp always needs medical treatment.

- Apply an antifungal over-the-counter cream such as clotrimazole to the skin patches. Within 7–10 days they should be clearing but continue treatment for a week after the last patches have gone.
- Always wash your hands after touching the child's ringworm and make sure that the child does the same. Keep towel and facecloth separate and wash

daily. Buy a new hairbrush and comb.
- Take a child with ringworm infection of the scalp to a doctor. The fungus lives in the hair roots, so creams are not enough to eradicate it. In addition, wash hair daily with a mild shampoo. There is no reason to have the hair cut.
- Have a pet treated if suspected as the source of infection.
- All pet bedding needs disinfecting or discarding. Vacuum floors and soft furnishings and restrict pets to rooms with washable floors.
- Not necessary to keep the child off school.

Medical treatment

For scalp ringworm, a doctor will prescribe the antifungal medication griseofulvin. A four- to eight-week course is likely to be needed to eradicate the infection. The doctor may also prescribe an antifungal shampoo and cream.

Looks like

Discoid eczema (see page 74). Psoriasis (see pages 82–83). Herald patch of pityriasis (see page 80).

How it is spread

Ringworm is transmitted by direct or transferred contact with fungal spores, often from a pet. Not very infectious.

Headlice

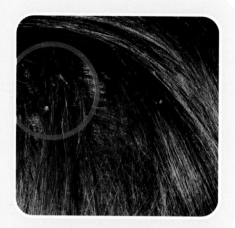

ABOVE: With headlice developing multiple resistance to insecticidal treatments, it's vital to follow local treatment regimes and only use insecticides on live lice.

Looks like
Possibly dandruff.

Note
Babies, pregnant and breastfeeding mothers should use wet combing. Shampoos are too dilute to work.

Chlorine interferes with the effect of some insecticides. Regular swimmers should wash their hair in a swimmer's shampoo and allow it to dry completely before treatment. Permethrin is claimed to be unaffected by chlorine.

What is it?
Headlice are insects, just visible to the naked eye, that live exclusively on the human scalp. They feed by sucking blood and crawl readily from head to head, regardless of the cleanliness of their host. They are usually an unsuspected visitor but, once in residence for some weeks, they can cause a characteristic itch, particularly around the margins of the hair. Any rash is red, at the hair margins and the nape of the neck.

Symptoms
At least one living and moving headlouse is required proof of infestation. Any other signs might point to a past visit.
- Moving insects the size of matchstick heads.
- Young lice grow from pinhead size.
- White flecks stuck firmly to the hair, usually near the scalp. These are nits, the shells of hatched lice. Unlike dandruff, which brushes out easily, nits stick fast to the hair.
- Itching, but only in a minority of children.
- Red rash on the back of the neck or hair margins caused by an allergy to the louse droppings.

What to do
- Inspect the child's hair using a fine-toothed detector comb. Wash the hair with a normal shampoo and apply conditioner. Untangle the hair with an ordinary comb. Run the detector comb right through the hair starting at the roots. Work systematically over the scalp.
- Check comb for lice after each stroke by wiping on kitchen paper.
- If live lice are found, check the entire family.
- Inform all contacts, including friends, babysitters, relatives, nursery and school staff.
- Treat everyone on whom lice are found either with an insecticide or by wet combing. Insecticides contain malathion or an insecticide called a pyrethroid – phenothrin or permethrin. Repeat in seven days. Young children and those with asthma, eczema or even a dry skin should use an insecticide that is water based, not alcohol based. Do not exceed the doses of insecticide stipulated by the manufacturer.
- Check the hair after treatment. Treatment failure is common. A mixture of adult (large) and baby (small) lice (which must have hatched on the child's head) is needed to prove treatment failure, rather than a new visit.
- Either try the alternative insecticide, repeating after a week, or wet comb.

Key signs
Rash and itch suggest long-standing infestation. Recent or short-lived infestation is far more common.

*** Infestation extremely common. The typical rash at the back of the neck is not common.

- If the second insecticide fails, either consult a doctor or wet comb.
- As a preventive, wet comb the child's hair at least weekly to remove any new lice.
- Keeping your child off nursery or school doesn't stop head lice from spreading. They can stay at school, but live lice must be treated.

Medical treatment
A doctor can prescribe a different insecticide containing carbaryl. This is available only on prescription because of theoretical concerns that it might cause cancer.

Complementary treatments
The insecticide-free method of clearing lice is called wet combing. It follows the same steps as wet combing for detection but requires a co-operative child and at least 20–30 minutes per session. Having inspected the entire head, sit the child upright with a towel round the shoulders but leaving the hair as wet as possible. Repeat the systematic section-by-section combing, clearing any lice off the comb as you find them. Repeat every three or four days for the next two weeks (five times in all) to catch any baby lice emerging from eggs.
Herbalism Products based on tea tree and other essential oils are widely available and popular. However, many essential oils used are listed as being harmful to children. Tea tree oil can be more toxic than either of the first-choice insecticides malathion and permethrin.

Louse life cycle
The louse lays eggs near the scalp and glues them to the base of a hair. Seven to ten days later the eggs hatch into pinhead-sized new lice, leaving the pearly white shell, or nit, stuck to the hair. The new louse grows, moulting three times over 7–14 days. It is then adult, ready to mate and lay new eggs.

Headlice – so what?
Apart from the irritant effect, lice are not harmful. They do not carry any particular diseases and, although in very large numbers lice can make a child feel unwell, this is extremely rare as most children have only a few. However, they are unpleasant and parents are expected to keep their family free of them.

Cold sores (fever blisters)

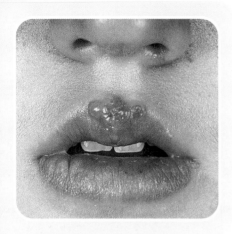

What is it?
Cold sores are caused by a virus (herpes simplex, not a cold virus) that, once caught, remains in the body for life. The first time the virus attacks, it does not cause cold sores. Although frequently unnoticed, it occasionally causes an influenza-like illness with painful mouth and lip ulcers. Only the first attack results from spread by skin contact, and transmission is by contact with infected fluid from blisters.

Once in the body the virus lies in a resting state at nerve junctions until it is re-awakened. The re-awakening – by a trigger such as a fever, viral infection, hot sun or a biting wind – causes a cold sore. Stress and being run down decrease resistance.

ABOVE: Over 90 per cent of people carry the herpes simplex virus that causes cold sores.

Symptoms
- A sore, itchy area near the mouth. This lasts for 24 hours.
- A small, clear blister surrounded by red appears. It rapidly crusts over.
- Blisters may appear in clusters.

What to do
- At the first tingly cold sore sensation, apply antiviral cold sore cream (aciclovir) or lotion. Repeat every four hours.
- Wash hands after touching the sore.
- Avoid kissing the child's mouth and don't let him or her kiss others.

In addition, or instead of antiviral treatment:
- Ease the tingle with a piece of wetted or frozen cotton wool held to the sore.
- Apply petroleum jelly (Vaseline) to prevent cracking.
- Give soft foods and offer a straw for drinking.
- Sterilize cutlery and cups after use and keep the child's facecloth and towel separate from those for the rest of the family.
- To help prevent repeat attacks apply lip balm or petroleum jelly to lips in cold weather, especially when the child has a cold or fever. In sunny weather, put on factor 25 or 30 sunblock.

There is no need for a child to stay off nursery or school. Cold sores are infectious, but infection in young children is almost universal.

Key signs
Painful blisters and crusts alone or in a cluster, most commonly near mouth or nose.

*** Very common.

Incubation
One to six days.

Medical treatment
Not usually needed. But consult a doctor if the child gets repeated attacks. A doctor can prescribe aciclovir cream to apply at the first symptoms. Consult a doctor if the child has atopic eczema and develops a cold sore because the herpes virus can produce an extremely unpleasant, sheet-like, studded rash and illness. A doctor will give aciclovir to take by mouth.

Outlook
The blister crusts over after one to two days and the scab falls off within 7–10 days. Scarring does not occur. Repeat attacks are likely.

Complementary treatments
Homoeopathy Arsen Alb 30c for itchy, swollen sores; Cantharis 30c for smarting, burning blisters; Nat Mur 30c for any blisters around mouth; Rhus Tox 30c when blisters tingle or itch angrily. Take Herpes Simplex nosode 30c for protection. Give four to six doses every three hours.
Herbalism Dab frequently with goldenseal tincture. Don't use goldenseal on under-twos. Drink chickweed, dandelion, puha, rosehip and/or parsley teas.

A small trial of six per cent tea tree gel on adults cleared cold sores as fast as aciclovir. Don't use tea tree oil on children under two.
Aromatherapy Dab geranium or rose oil on to the sores. Always dilute essential oils in a carrier oil first. Always check your child for sensitivity first, by putting oil on his or her skin and observing for 24 hours.

Looks like
Impetigo (see page 60).

How it is spread
The blister itself, the fluid inside and the child's saliva all carry infection. The virus is highly infectious. At any one time, one young child in five has this virus in his or her saliva.

Scabies

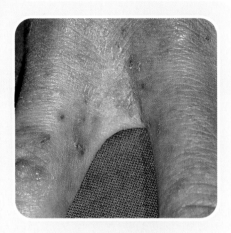

What is it?
An infestation by a scarcely visible mite (Sarcoptes scabiei) that burrows into the skin. The mites lay 2–3 eggs a day in the skin burrows. Baby mites hatch out, crawl out onto the skin and create new burrows. Scabies is a nuisance but not serious.

The intense itch caused by an allergic reaction to the saliva or droppings of the mite causes scratching, often introducing a secondary infection. Scabies has a 30- to 50-year cycle, now close to its peak. At the peak, the scabies mite becomes more active, infecting people who would have been unaffected in the past.

ABOVE: The female scabies mite usually burrows under loose skin folds, such as between the fingers, where she lays 2–3 eggs a day.

How it is spread
By skin-to-skin contact, often involving holding hands, sharing a bed or other direct contact. Outbreaks of scabies sometimes occur in nurseries. The person is infectious for up to a month before the rash and itch emerge, but is no longer infectious 24 hours after starting treatment.

Symptoms
- Rubbing and scratching especially in bed at night or after a bath.
- Intensely itchy, variable rash of small bumps, red spots, tiny blisters, scabs and scaly eczema-like patches. Most common between fingers, on hands and wrists, on feet, in armpits and groin, although any part of the body can be affected. Head and face are usually spared.
- In babies, unlike in adults, the face, scalp and neck can be affected.
- The itchy rash can take four to six weeks to develop.
- Itch intensifies at night and in heat.
- Other people in the family may be affected.
- Fine meandering lines occasionally visible near the rash.

What to do
Keep the child off nursery or school. Contact a doctor. The following steps are supplementary to their treatment.
- Contact everyone in household contact with the family in the past two months. Everyone needs treatment, ideally on the same day, even without signs of scabies.
- Note exactly where the rash is. To be certain that treatment has been effective, any new spots must be noted.
- Itch and the rash can continue and even get worse for four to six weeks. This does not mean that the treatment has failed. Soothe the itch with calamine or antihistamine cream and keep the child cool.
- Wash all clothes worn in the past week, trainers, bedlinen and towels on a hot wash, dry in a hot dryer or sunlight, and iron. Perfectly clean clothes do not need re-laundering. Otherwise, re-wash.
- Ask doctor about an insecticide spray for unwashable items such as shoes and belts. Alternatively, bag them in plastic and leave somewhere cool for two weeks to starve mites to death.
- Treatment of furnishings, carpets and pets is not needed. As a

Key signs
Intensely itchy rash, with variable rash of bumps, spots and blisters often on the hands and feet.

** Common.

Incubation
7–27 days.

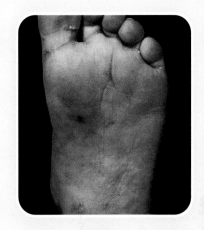

precaution, however, vacuum the whole house.
- Once away from a human body, mites die after 72 hours.
- Child can return to school once treatment has started.

Medical treatments
- A doctor will prescribe an insecticide cream or lotion. Follow instructions for application carefully.
- Dermatologists say that one key reason why treatment often fails is that contacts don't take scabies seriously and don't apply treatments. Another reason is that creams and lotions are not applied according to manufacturers' instructions.
- If your child finds that the treatment prescribed by your doctor stings, ask for permethrin cream which is usually mild. It is also safe for pregnant and breastfeeding women.
- Repeat treatment after seven days.
- Babies and children under two, as well as people on whom previous treatment has failed, need to

apply lotion or cream to the scalp, neck, face and ears, as well as the body.
- Crusted spots may be infected and require an antibiotic.
- The doctor may take skin scrapings and examine them under light microscopy to reveal mites.

Complementary treatments
Complementary treatments should supplement conventional medical treatment, not replace it.
Aromatherapy Treat frequently with one to two drops of tea tree (over-twos), clove, lavender, thyme and/or peppermint oil in base of soya/almond oil.
Homoeopathy Sulphur 30c, twice a day for up to three days; Arsen Alb 6c when warmth intensifies itch.
Herbalism Tansy tincture or infusion in bath water.

Looks like
Contact dermatitis (see pages 72–73).
Atopic eczema (see pages 68–71).

Impetigo

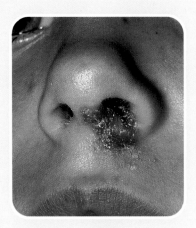

Key signs
Crops of itchy yellowy blisters and crusted sores usually around nose and mouth.

** Common.

Infectious?
Children are infectious while the sores are discharging or until two days after starting treatment.

Looks like
Cold sores (see pages 56–57).

How it is spread
Impetigo is highly contagious. It is spread by direct or transferred contact with the sores.

Symptoms
- Tiny blisters on reddened skin, especially around the nose and mouth. Blisters sometimes appear on the neck or hands.
- Within 24 hours the blisters break, exposing a patch that oozes a cloudy yellow liquid. Over four to six days this forms a honey-gold crust.
- Blisters may join together in unsightly clusters.
- As impetigo heals, it leaves rings of reddened skin.

What to do
Consult a doctor to check the diagnosis and start antibiotic treatment. The following steps are supplementary.
- Bathe the sores using antibacterial soap. Alternatively, sprinkle salt into warm water. Soak the sores in kitchen paper impregnated with the salt solution. Dab dry.
- Be scrupulous about hygiene. Wash the child's hands frequently and your own if bathing the sores.

What is it?
A bacterial infection most common on the face and hands. Impetigo is usually caused by a bacterium infecting the skin through a cut or sore, then spreading to unaffected skin. Staphylococcus aureus, which normally lives on the skin and in the nose, is the most common agent.

- Keep the child's facecloth and towel separate from those of the rest of the family and wash daily with their sheet and/or pillowcase on the hottest wash cycle.
- Bathe the child separately from the rest of the family.
- Dissuade the child from touching the crusts.
- Trim nails short.

Medical treatment
- Antibiotic ointment kills the bacteria and softens the crusts.
- It is usually applied three to four times a day for seven days.
- Antibiotics by mouth are given if ointment isn't effective or the outbreak is severe. This clears impetigo in four to five days.
- The child must normally stay off school until the crusts have dried.

Complementary treatments
Herbalism Dab frequently with calendula ointment or lotion.
Aromatherapy Dilute two drops of tea tree or thyme oil in three teaspoons of olive or soya oil and apply directly. Don't use tea tree on children under two.

Molluscum

What is it?
An infection similar to warts, but caused by a different virus.

Common in pre-school children. The spots are fairly contagious and can spread easily from one skin surface to another by contact. Molluscum is more common in children with allergies, and with eczema in particular. Their molluscum spots last longer and are more numerous.

Key signs
Waxy, wart-like spots in clusters or alone.

** Common.

Incubation
6–12 weeks.

Symptoms
- Small, soft, pearly or waxy, flesh-coloured or white spots, sometimes with a central dip like a yew berry.
- Spots measure 1–5mm (up to ¼in) across.
- Skin immediately around spots can be reddened or darkened.
- Spots most common on soft skin of trunk, thighs, bottom, face and hands, or less commonly on palms and soles.
- Spots may itch.
- Spots may redden and become inflamed as the body fights the virus.
- Occasionally, eczema-like patches surround the spots.

What to do
- Consult a doctor who can confirm the diagnosis and certify that the child can continue to attend nursery or school.
- As molluscum resolves naturally, the spots occasionally flare up and become inflamed. Consult your doctor if this occurs because

the inflamed spots can leave scars.
- In the great majority of cases no treatment is called for.
- If you want to speed these spots on their way, massage them very gently with tweezers until the cheesy-white centre comes out, usually followed by a drop of blood. Wipe clean and dab on a spot of antiseptic.
- If possible, do this while the child is asleep to cause minimum disruption.
- Make sure the child does not share facecloths or towels.
- The child can attend nursery or school. Molluscum is not a serious condition.

Medical treatment
Rarely needed. If necessary, molluscum responds to light cryotherapy (freezing).

Outlook
The spots will disappear naturally, usually within a few months. Occasionally they may persist for a year or two.

How it is spread
Direct contact with spots or indirectly by touching clothes, bedding, towels, etc. Moderately infectious in families.

Warts

Key signs
Firm, painless lumps most often on backs of hands and fingers.

** Common, but not in children under two.

Incubation
1–20 months.

Looks like
Molluscum (see page 61).

How it is spread
By direct person-to-person contact or self-infection.

A scratched wart sheds viral particles. However, the virus is not especially infectious.

Symptoms
- Thickened lumps in the skin, several millimetres (up to ¼in) across, with a rough, horny surface.
- Clumps of warts look like cauliflower florets.
- Tiny black spots in the centre of the wart are blood vessels.

What to do
Consult a doctor to confirm the diagnosis. A wart that is unsightly or in an awkward place may warrant treatment.
- Treatment may be a lotion, gel or plaster, and demands patience and persistence. Salicylic acid is the most successful home treatment but requires accurate application.
- Soak the skin in warm water for two to three minutes and pat dry. Rub down the wart with an emery board or wet and dry sandpaper. Gels stay on the wart, but if using a lotion, cover the surrounding skin with a corn plaster or an ordinary plaster with a hole punched through. Apply the

lotion or gel and allow to dry.
- Repeat daily, rubbing down the surface of the wart.
- The child should only use his or her own sponge, facecloth and towel.
- Your child can attend school. Warts may need covering for activities involving skin-to-skin contact.

What is it?
Warts are growths caused by the human papilloma virus. They consist of infected skin cells. They have no roots, are not cancerous and are harmless. They are easier to recognize than to treat.

Medical treatment
If warts persist after 12 weeks, consult a doctor. Liquid nitrogen freezing is possible but painful for young children. However, light freezes may be all that's needed. After treatment a blister forms and lifts the wart off.

Outlook
Fifty per cent of warts vanish within a year and 90 per cent within two years. The immune system fights off the virus and the wart vanishes, leaving the child with good immunity.

Verrucas

Key signs
Firm circular growths on soles or sides of feet.

*** Common in school-age children.

Incubation
1–20 months.

What is it?
Verrucas (plantar warts) are warts on the feet. They consist of dead skin cells. Caused by the human papilloma virus, they can be difficult to treat. Eventually almost all disappear.

Symptoms
- Small round lumps/circles on foot. Usually white, flesh coloured or brown. Minute black dots on the verruca are tiny blood vessels and distinguish a verruca from a corn.
- May appear in floret-like clusters. This is a mosaic verruca.
- Usually painless, but hurt if squeezed or pinched

What to do
If confident with the diagnosis, verrucas can safely be treated at home. Otherwise, consult a doctor or chiropodist.

Home treatments are irritant, drying or caustic. The most effective is salicylic acid either as an impregnated plaster, paint or gel. Prepare skin by soaking foot in warm water for two to three minutes and rubbing down verruca with a pumice stone or wet and dry sandpaper. Apply paint/gel accurately, avoiding surrounding skin. Allow to dry. Some gels form a watertight seal. Otherwise cover with a waterproof plaster. Repeat

daily for 12 weeks or until verruca disappears.

Your child can attend nursery or school. The school may require the verruca to be covered for swimming and barefoot activities.

Medical treatment
If home treatment fails, consult a doctor who may refer your child to a chiropodist. As most verrucas disappear within a year many health professionals suggest no treatment. Others believe that they are worth treating to avoid spreading infection and because they can be painful. Apart from salicylic acid treatment, the verruca can be pared with a scalpel or frozen with liquid nitrogen using a cryogun. This is very painful for young children, although using an anaesthetic cream helps. Lasers are popular but the evidence that they help is scant.

A last resort is to use electrocautery and surgical curettage, where the verruca is scraped and burnt out. These methods can leave permanent scars.

Looks like
Corns.

How it is spread
By contact. Infection is more likely through damaged or water-soaked skin.

Non-contagious rashes

Diagnosis

A child with a rash or other skin condition, but no other signs of being unwell, is not likely to be seriously unwell. Many rashes that are not spread by contact or by an illness that makes your child generally unwell (see Rashes with fever, page 32) are a sign of either a local reaction to an irritant or an infection, or else an allergic reaction.

A child with a skin condition that does not clear up quickly should see a doctor, especially if he or she is uncomfortable or upset by the rash. It's important to let a doctor see an unexplained skin condition as it may be the earliest or most obvious sign of a disease affecting multiple organs or even of a nutritional deficiency.

For rashes that appear after a cause you have reason to suspect, see
Contact dermatitis
Insect bites
Plant rashes
Polymorphic light eruption
Sunburn
Vaccine rashes

For spots or rashes on the face or mouth only, see
Angio-oedema
Lick eczema

For conditions affecting the feet only, see
Glazed foot

For itchy rashes anywhere on the body, see
Contact dermatitis
Discoid eczema
Atopic eczema
Erythema multiforme
Polymorphic light eruption
Psoriasis
Chickenpox
Thrush
Urticaria

For rashes that affect skin colour, see
Vitiligo

For infected spots, see
Boils

For blistering rashes, see
Plant rashes
Chickenpox

For spots and rashes that are sore but not itchy, see
Boils
Insect bites
Lick eczema
Polymorphic light eruption
Sunburn
Thrush
Glazed foot

For pink-red spots and patches, see
Contact dermatitis
Discoid eczema
Atopic eczema
Erythema multiforme
Pityriasis rosea
Psoriasis
Urticaria
Vaccine rashes

Vitiligo

What is it?

A disfiguring but harmless problem where all brown pigment is lost, leaving irregular areas of white skin. The pigment cells, melanocytes, disappear. The cause is thought to be an autoimmune disorder (which causes the body to attack its own tissues), leading to pigment cell destruction. Vitiligo often runs in families and is more common in children with other autoimmune disorders, particularly those affecting the thyroid.

Vitiligo is more common in girls and, although it affects children of any skin colour, it appears to be more common in dark-skinned children.

Symptoms

- Pale or white patches, often on both sides of the body.
- Usually first on the face, particularly around the mouth; later affects any area.
- Pale skin sometimes surrounded by especially dark skin.
- More frequent on parts of the body that tend to get rubbed.
- Hair on a patch of vitiligo eventually turns white.

What to do

- Protect pale skin against sunshine using a high-factor sunblock.
- Consult a doctor for diagnosis.
- Keep the child out of the sunshine to mask the condition in a fair-skinned child.
- Use a self-tanning or tinted sunblock on obvious patches.

Key signs

Irregular flat patches of pale skin, often affecting both sides of the body.

* Uncommon.

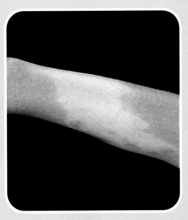

Medical treatment

- If very disfiguring, a very strong steroid cream can be tried as treatment for new patches. Darkening is not guaranteed or complete, but the patches may look much better after treatment.
- Professional camouflage for exposed areas.

Outlook

While vitiligo is developing it is impossible to know how far it will spread. Rapid skin colour loss is often followed by stability. Eventually the colour loss stops and in some children the colour improves considerably. Children regain their skin colour more often than adults.

The outlook is best for younger children, those with dark skins and children with isolated vitiligo on the face.

Complementary treatment

Although there is some early evidence that cognitive-behavioural therapy slows down spread of vitiligo in adults, no research has been conducted yet in children.

Looks like

Fungal skin infection. Temporary pale skin patches after healing of another skin disorder, such as eczema.

Atopic eczema

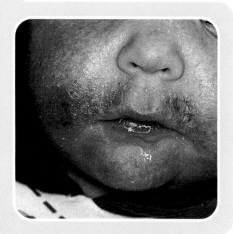

What is it?
Atopic eczema is an inflammatory skin condition that causes an itchy red rash. It is the most common skin problem in young children, affecting 15–20 per cent of children regardless of the colour of their skin. Most children who are going to develop eczema do so before the age of two and certainly before five.

ABOVE: For any infant with severe facial eczema that is worse after sleep, parents should take steps to eliminate house-dust mite from bedding by using a foam mattress and covering it with an anti-allergy cover, vacuuming at least weekly and reducing soft toy numbers in and near the cot.

What causes it?
In most children eczema is caused by a genetic tendency to allergy, although one child in five who has eczema has no other signs of allergy. There is a strong inherited tendency, so it is quite likely that other family members are also affected.

For eczema to develop, however, environmental factors are needed as well as susceptibility. It is usually impossible to pinpoint the trigger that starts eczema in a particular baby, but it may be contact with house dust, animal fur or pollen, or all of them. Overheating, dry air, cold weather, coarse cloth, especially wool next to the skin, and very possibly hard tap water make eczema worse and so do teething, colds and other infections. In babies under one, certain foods can aggravate eczema.

Children often scratch the wildly itchy spots and cause secondary infections, leading to large weepy and crusty areas of skin.

Symptoms
- Patches of rough, red itchy skin on the face and arms. These may spread, affecting the skin creases at the wrists, elbows and knees. Sometimes skin all over the body becomes dry and rough.
- Pimples, blisters and cracks appear on the affected areas, as well as crusting, swelling and scaling.
- The rash is usually mild – just one or two red, dry and flaky patches – but is occasionally severe, involving large areas of sore and weeping skin.
- A baby, often between 3 and 18 months, becomes restless, sleeping poorly and rubbing his or her face
- In black children, the patches of eczema may look paler or darker than the surrounding skin.
- In severely affected areas, the skin becomes thick and tough.

What to do
- Keep the baby's skin hydrated by applying a moisturizer (emollient) such as 50 per cent white soft paraffin with 50 per cent liquid paraffin. Use at least twice a day, including once after an evening bath or shower. Emollients help to seal in the skin's natural moisture, protect the skin against allergens

and irritants, and soothe inflammation. Before eating, apply emollient to exposed areas of skin, such as a baby's face and hands.

- Stop using soap and bubble bath. Wash instead with a soap substitute such as aqueous cream.
- Aqueous cream is a light emollient. Greasier preparations include white soft paraffin, emulsifying ointment, and liquid and white soft paraffin ointment. Children with black skin need an extra-rich emollient ointment, such as cocoa butter or preservative-free yellow soft paraffin.
- Discourage scratching. To limit damage, keep nails short and at night dress a small child in an all-in-one sleepsuit with attached mittens.
- Improve the child's sleep by reducing overnight itching. Moisturize the skin well before bed, keep the bedroom cool at 10–16°C (50–60°F), use sheets rather than a duvet and light, cool nightclothes. Soft synthetic materials are as good as cotton, but avoid rough materials and scratchy seams. If the child wakes scratching, cool the skin with moisturizer and give a cold drink.
- Restrict access of furry or feathered pets to a limited part of the house – such as the kitchen because this room usually has fewer soft furnishings and no carpet and so is easier to keep clean.
- Keep the house-dust mite at bay by wet-wiping bedrooms and vacuuming frequently, ideally with a high-filtration cleaner. Keep soft toys, soft furnishings and carpets to a minimum.

Key signs
An itchy, dry red rash often predominantly on the face and arms in babies but involving the wrists, the insides of the elbows and the backs of the knees in toddlers and older children. Many babies also have dry skin.

✱✱✱ Very common.

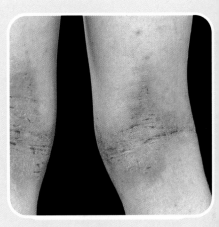

A weekly overnight spell in the freezer kills any mites in soft toys.

- Choose absorbent, non-irritating materials such as cotton or soft synthetics. White clothes show up stains from creams and dark clothes show skin flakes. Choose long, baggy styles with seams that don't rub and long sleeves and legs. Use light, soft cotton or synthetic bedding.
- Try non-biological or sensitive skin washing powders until you find one that suits your child's skin. Wash new clothes to remove irritants before use.
- Wash and cream the child's hands after he plays with sand, playdough or water. Teach him always to do this himself.
- Only use antibacterial products (containing benzalkonium chloride, triclosan) during a flare-up when infection is present.
- Recent research has highlighted a possible link between eczema and later peanut allergy. The suggestion is that peanut oils in emollients used by children with eczema could sensitize them to

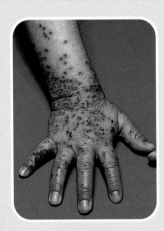

ABOVE: **Children with eczema are vulnerable to viral skin infections. The herpes simplex virus that causes cold sores can trigger eczema herpeticum, causing the rapid spread of a typically studded rash.**

peanuts. The research currently does, however, appear conflicting. To be on the safe side, avoid skin products containing groundnut or arachis (peanut) oil.

- To identify a food that could be triggering the eczema, keep a food diary. Stopping a child from eating foods without clear evidence that they definitely trigger eczema flare-ups is pointless and potentially harmful. Your child may be the exception, but the rule is that foods don't trigger eczema.

Medical treatment

- A doctor can prescribe both emollient skin preparations and, if nights remain very disturbed, a sedating antihistamine medicine to break the itch–scratch cycle.
- Steroid creams speed up the healing of skin damaged by eczema. Lotions and creams are used on weeping sores, and ointments on dry eczema, although some dermatologists prefer ointments for all areas. A mild cream, such as one per cent hydrocortisone, is tried first, progressing to a moderate strength for short spells if needed. Mild creams are generally prescribed for delicate skin such as on the face, armpits and nappy area, whereas thicker skin such as the palms and soles may need a moderate strength. Only the small quantities shown by the doctor or nurse should be used, and only on affected areas. Steroid preparations are generally applied for 10–14 days while the eczema is active.
- Children with severe eczema often appear to get much better with wet wrapping, a technique

that involves a health professional (and, after instruction, a parent) coating the skin thickly with moisturizers before wrapping the child in layers of moist bandage. Some children need short spells of continuous wet wrapping, whereas others only need it at night.

- If the child's skin has developed a secondary infection, a doctor will prescribe antibiotics.
- Diet is rarely a cause of eczema but a doctor or dietitian can advise on changes to what your child eats.
- Rarely, very severe eczema may require immune-suppressant drugs, including ciclosporin, or ultraviolet light therapy.
- Other immune suppressants that work in a similar way to ciclosporin, including ascomycin, are being tried in hospital dermatology departments, but are not yet licensed for use in eczema. Tacrolimus will soon be available for severe atopic eczema.

Outlook

Most children outgrow eczema by their teens. Meanwhile, it lasts for months or years, with spells of improvement and exacerbation. The children most likely to outgrow it are those who developed it only mildly on limited parts of the body, and those who developed it later and had no family history of eczema or other allergic conditions.

Complementary treatments

The effectiveness of evening primrose oil in improving eczema on a long-term basis is controversial. A doctor can prescribe capsules to be added to a baby's feeds.

Traditional herbal medicines Research into their effectiveness is conflicting and clouded by recent discoveries that some creams and ointments contain steroids. If you do try traditional medicines for your child, only buy clearly labelled products, show them first to your doctor and preferably consult a qualified practitioner. The Chinese treatments involving infusions frequently taste so bitter that children refuse them.

Salt water baths, using sea salt at the concentration you would find in the sea, twice a week, may help, especially if your child's eczema tends to get infected. An old-fashioned remedy is to dissolve three 500ml (1 pint) jugfuls of sea salt in 40 litres (9 gallons) of water or enough for your child to soak in. Caution: this can sting open sores.

Massage reduces stress, boosts your parent–child relationship and may stimulate the circulation. So long as the massage is restricted to areas of unbroken skin, it certainly does no harm! However, it's better to use emollients rather than carrier oils for massage. One study suggests that massaged children cope with their eczema better and are less anxious.

Aromatherapy Caution: carrier oils and aromatherapy oils can provoke a reaction in children with eczema. Never use aromatherapy oils neat and test carrier oils on a discreet area for 24 hours before use. Almond or grapeseed oil is most likely to be tolerated. A small study suggests that what counts is not the essential oil used but the touch and counselling.

Hypnotherapy and relaxation may help children to break the damaging itch–scratch cycle.

Homoeopathy Consult a medically qualified homoeopath who will prescribe either a general constitutional remedy to boost the child's immune responses, followed by a pathological remedy to complete treatment, or will prescribe individually tailored constitutional remedies. Note that children with eczema and asthma require expert treatment. These remedies are general suggestions only: Arsen Alb 6c for dry, itching and burning eczema and thickened skin; Graphites 6c for raw, cracked, sticky and scabby patches of eczema; Nat Mur 6C when eczema is raw and inflamed; Psorinum 6c for night itching and eczema in skin creases at joints; Rhus Tox 6c for intense itching and tingling; Sulphur 6c for dry, scaly patches or eczema that easily becomes infected.

If symptoms get worse, stop remedy immediately.

Shiatsu Stress exacerbates eczema and shiatsu aids relaxation. So does reflexology.

Herbalism Camomile cream and goldenseal preparations are soothing, but check first with your doctor or practice nurse before using a herbal cream for a child with eczema.

Ayurvedic medicine Tincture of neem leaf has anti-inflammatory and antifungal properties. Traditionally, poultices and pastes have been used to treat eczema.

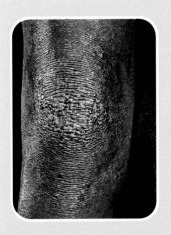

ABOVE: **Constant scratching thickens and coarsens the skin of children with chronic eczema. Recent sores leave obvious patches of dark or light skin in children with a black skin.**

Contact dermatitis

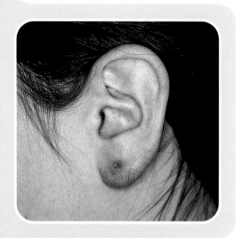

ABOVE: Nickel allergy from cheap ear rings produces soreness and swelling that can take weeks to fully resolve. Even when the skin looks normal it is still vulnerable. Sterling silver earrings do not cause the same reaction and are scarcely more expensive than nickel.

What is it?
Contact dermatitis is an inflammation of the skin caused by an irritant or an allergic reaction. Both reactions are common, but in children irritant contact dermatitis is more likely.

What causes it?
Irritant contact dermatitis is very common and can affect anyone. It is especially common in children with eczema whose skin is already damaged. Once it is damaged, the skin's ability to protect is undermined and it can easily be irritated further. A vicious cycle then develops that can be hard to break. The irritant is either something mild but frequently in contact with the skin or something strong, such as ammonia. Ammonia released in a wet nappy can cause the type of contact dermatitis better known as nappy rash (see pages 30–31). Water, detergents and chemicals can all act as irritants.

Allergic contact dermatitis affects children who develop an allergic response to a particular substance. Allergic reactions can take a long time (years) to develop and are usually lifelong. The area of skin affected is usually that in contact with the allergen, but the inflammation may spread further. Fragrances, rubber, preservatives in skin creams, medicated creams and ointments, and sunscreens can cause allergies. Nickel (in buttons on jeans, zips, cheap ear rings and watch straps) is a common allergen. Other common sensitizers include hand lotions, make-up and deodorants. Rubber can provoke a reaction in some children. Elastic at waists and wrists creates problems; so can stretchy crepe bandages. Some children have quite specific and unusual reactions, e.g. to poster paints. The lanolins used in medications and toiletries are now of improved quality and purity and are less likely to cause allergic reactions.

Symptoms
- An itchy, red rash at the point of contact with the irritant or allergen.
- Flaking or blistering. The blisters break or are scratched open and form crusts.
- Scratched or rubbed skin thickens and becomes wrinkled and dry.

Key signs
Itchy sore red rash, sometimes flaky or with cracked skin or tiny blisters, frequently at specific points on the body that suggest an external cause.

*** Very common.

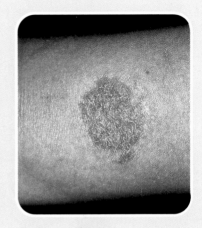

What to do
- Identify the source of the trouble. If at all possible, avoid it. If that is not possible, make sure the irritant does not come into direct contact with the skin. Encourage a young child to wear an all-in-one or an older girl to wear a body suit under jeans.
- Avoid any products that are likely to irritate the skin even more – especially bubble baths and highly scented soaps.
- While the rash is clearing up be careful to avoid using soap or any other foaming product on the affected area. Use aqueous cream or plain tap water instead and shower the child in preference to bathing. Then apply emollient cream generously, especially if the rash is itchy.
- Instead of biological washing powders, use the non-biological alternative or a powder prepared for sensitive skins.
- Dress the child in soft, cool clothes.

Medical treatment
If the rash continues for a week after you are certain you have removed all sources of contact, consult a doctor.

The doctor may prescribe a mild corticosteroid cream to ease the itchy discomfort, reduce the inflammation and soothe the irritated skin. If the rash has become infected, an antibiotic cream will clear it.

Outlook
The rash will clear and should not spread, although complete recovery may take some weeks. Recovery can take longer if contact with the irritant or allergen has continued for a long time.

Complementary treatment
Herbalism Soothe inflamed skin with camomile cream, calendula lotion, aloe vera gel or vitamin E oil. Check first with your health visitor or doctor before using herbal products on a child with contact dermatitis.

Discoid eczema

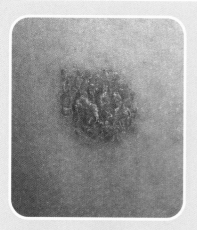

Key signs
Circles of scaly eczema, sometimes accompanied by eczema on other parts of the body.

* Uncommon.

Looks like
Ringworm (see page 53).

Symptoms
- Circular eczema patches about the size of a coin, particularly on the arms and legs.
- Unaffected skin may be normal, but is sometimes dry.
- Eczema may be distributed elsewhere over the body.
- The patches are usually very itchy.

What to do
- Protect the child's skin from injury. Dress in clothes with long sleeves and legs.
- Start moisturizing treatment as soon as discoid eczema appears. Try different products until you find one that suits the child.
- Consult a doctor. The diagnosis is not always clear.

What is it?
Also called nummular dermatitis, this condition may be more common in patients with a history of atopic eczema. A trigger is rarely identifiable, although a minor injury, insect bite or sting may act as the stimulus. Discoid eczema does not appear to run in families and is not associated with other allergic conditions such as asthma. Discoid eczema is more resistant to treatment and the skin appears drier than in atopic eczema (see pages 68–71).

Medical treatment
Anti-inflammatory steroid creams and ointments reduce any irritation and clear the eczema. Treatment is usually needed once or twice a day for two weeks and the course may be repeated.

Eczema flares that do not improve with steroid treatment may be infected. This is more likely if sores are red and weeping.

Antibiotics are needed to clear a secondary infection.

Outlook
Discoid eczema clears by the same age as atopic eczema, with most children clear by age 11 and many much sooner. In some children it may be chronic.

Skin may appear darkened or lightened by discoid eczema, but marks fade eventually and permanent scars are rare.

Lick eczema

What is it?
Lick eczema (lip eczema) is a local form of irritant contact dermatitis. The child usually has a nervous or absent-minded habit of running the tongue round the mouth. This causes chafing and soreness and opens the skin up to irritation by other substances, especially food. Yeast extracts and other salty foods then irritate and inflame the area around the mouth.

Key signs
Chapped red area round the mouth. Lips may be cracked.

** Common.

Caution
Children with lick eczema are at increased risk of getting cold sores (see pages 56–57).

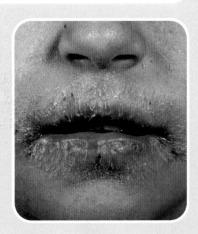

Symptoms
- Dry, chapped and red area around the lips.
- The sore area is often worst in the middle of the upper lip, but can extend around the whole mouth.
- Sometimes a narrow band of unaffected skin surrounds the lips.
- Sometimes, cracked lips.

What to do
- Encourage the child to stop licking his or her lips.
- Smear aqueous cream or white soft paraffin (Vaseline) round the mouth to protect the skin. This tastes unpleasant, so it acts as a deterrent.
- Protect the child's face with emollient before meals and before teeth cleaning.
- Always protect the child's face with an emollient in winter and in raw weather.

Medical treatment
A steroid cream can speed healing but is usually unnecessary.

Outlook
Lick eczema resolves within days once the child gets out of the habit of licking his or her lips.

Looks like
Food allergy.

Urticaria

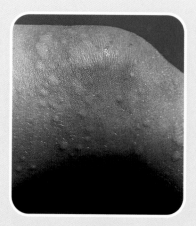

Looks Like
Erythema multiforme (see opposite).

Key signs
A sudden rash of itchy red or white weals that fade and move over minutes to hours.

** Common.

Caution
Angio-oedema (see page 78) and, rarely, anaphylaxis can develop with noisy or difficult breathing, swelling of the face or neck, puffy eyes and anxious behaviour.

Symptoms
- White, yellow or red, slightly raised weals of different shapes, often surrounded by inflammation.
- Itching, usually.
- After a few minutes or hours the weals fade or change shape. Others may replace them.
- Sometimes deeper swelling, especially on face (angio-oedema).

What to do
So long as the rash does not cause any swelling on the face, simply observe it carefully and cool it or dab on calamine to ease itching. You can give chlorphenamine syrup, obtainable without prescription. Try to think about events shortly before the rash appeared and identify the cause. This is often easier in children than in adults.

Some possibilities are: an allergen, such as nuts including peanuts, fish, eggs, strawberries and dairy foods; an antibiotic such as penicillin; a wasp or bee sting. Non-allergic stimuli include some food dyes (E102, tartrazine) or benzoate

What is it?
Urticaria (hives, nettlerash) is a sudden skin reaction to a stimulus that is sometimes an allergen, but not always. Children with or without a tendency to develop allergies react to a wide range of substances and circumstances. Urticaria can be short-lived (acute), chronic (lasting more than six weeks) or physical (a reaction to something in contact with the skin).

preservatives; cold, heat, sunlight or water; some drugs. The cause of physical urticaria is often clear. Physical urticaria causes include heat, sunlight and pressure against the skin. Stinging nettles, hairy caterpillars and animal saliva are other causes.

Medical treatment
Often not necessary. A doctor can prescribe an antihistamine medicine to reduce the rash and itching.

If the child develops anaphylactic shock (see Caution), contact a doctor urgently or, if not available, call your emergency medical number. The doctor can give the child an injection of adrenaline. Children prone to anaphylaxis should carry an adrenaline supply.

Outlook
Urticaria usually disappears within a few days, but in a minority of children can last for weeks. The few children who develop chronic urticaria are more likely to have other atopic conditions such as eczema, asthma or hayfever.

Erythema multiforme

What is it?
An uncommon condition of uncertain cause, although in at least half the cases the virus that causes cold sores (herpes simplex) is involved. It produces well-defined 'target' circles with a raised central red or sometimes purplish centre. The underlying cause may be an immune reaction to a virus, a fungal infection, an antibiotic or other drug treatment.

Key signs
Variable rash, often of circular spots with raised red or purplish 'target' centres.

* Uncommon.

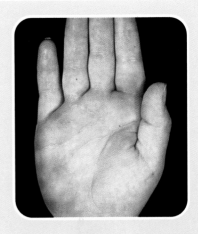

Symptoms
- The first sign of the rash may be a cold sore.
- Over four to five days, a rash evolves. 'Target' spots appear, especially on the hands and feet. The rash affects both sides of the body symmetrically.
- Rash spreads. The spots may itch. The eyes, mouth and other mucous membranes may become sore and red.
- The rash can occasionally be severe and spread very fast, making the child feverish and distinctly unwell. If the child develops sores or blisters on the mucus lining of their lips, eyes or anus, contact a doctor.

What to do
- Treat child as for a cold.
- Antihistamine medicine (such as chlorphenamine or promethazine) will ease the irritation.
- Contact a doctor if the rash spreads fast or the child becomes very unwell.
- Children who suffer repeated attacks of erythema multiforme linked with cold sores should in future apply aciclovir cream at the first sign of a cold sore.

Medical treatment
- Aciclovir cream applied as a preventive may suppress repeat attacks of erythema multiforme associated with herpes simplex.
- Antibiotics are usually given at the first sign of infection.

Outlook
Erythema multiforme usually heals naturally in two to four weeks. When linked with herpes simplex infection, it tends to recur.

Looks like
Urticaria (see opposite).

How it is caused
May be triggered by herpes simplex (cold sore virus), other viruses, infections or drugs.

Angio-oedema

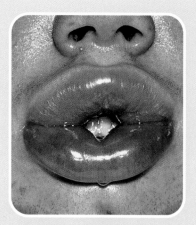

Key signs
An acute allergic reaction in which deeper skin layers and tissues just beneath the skin swell. Often seen together with urticaria (see page 76).

* Uncommon.

Symptoms
- Acute swelling, often of the face, particularly around the eyes and mouth.
- Frequently an urticarial rash as well.
- Unlike urticaria, angio-oedema is not itchy but it may be painful.
- Rarely, angio-oedema can affect the tissues lining the throat and airways, leading to noisy or difficult breathing and difficulty swallowing.

Caution
Angio-oedema may occasionally affect tissues inside the mouth and throat. At the first sign of anxiety, wheezing or difficult breathing, call an ambulance or your emergency medical number. Give any medication a child with a known allergy has to take in case of an attack. Calm and reassure the child until the ambulance arrives.

What is it?
Angio-oedema is an acute reaction that rapidly follows contact with, eating or even just breathing in a substance to which the child is sensitive. The reaction takes the same underlying form as urticaria, but involves the deeper layers of the skin and the tissues beneath it. It looks alarming, especially when the eyes or mouth swell. Although angio-oedema requires urgent action, it is usually not serious. However, on rare occasions, it can be life threatening.

What to do
- Consult a doctor if this is the child's first reaction.
- Be vigilant for further symptoms (see Caution).
- Try to identify the cause.

Medical treatment
Contact a doctor urgently or if not available call your emergency medical number. The doctor can give the child antihistamines and, if needed, an injection of adrenaline. Children prone to this reaction should carry an adrenaline supply.

For a rare form of hereditary angio-oedema, which occurs without urticaria, preventive treatment can be given.

Outlook
Angio-oedema usually settles in a few days, but occasionally causes a severe reaction (see Caution).

Polymorphic light eruption

What is it?
An inflammatory rash caused by an abnormal sensitivity to sunlight. It is thought to be an abnormal immune reaction to an allergen induced in the skin by ultraviolet (both UVA and UVB) rays. Polymorphic light eruption is more common in children with allergic disorders. It can run in families and affects children of all skin colours; it is more common in girls. The rash can take many forms, but individual children usually react in the same way each time.

Symptoms
- Itchy, burning red rash on skin exposed to sunshine.
- Blisters and spots within the rash.
- Occasionally, target ('bull's eye') spots.
- Affects arms and legs, face, tops of the feet, chest.
- Appears within minutes to four to six hours of exposure to sun. Occasionally does not appear for one or two days.
- Rash spreads and becomes more severe if re-exposed to sunshine.

What to do
Ensure child covers up or wears high-factor sunscreen with maximum UVA protection on bare skin when outdoors from spring onwards.

Key signs
Spotty pink, burning rash on sun-exposed skin coincides with the first strong sunshine of spring.

* Uncommon.

Caution
Sunlight through windows can cause polymorphic light eruption. Glass blocks ultraviolet B (UVB) but not UVA rays.

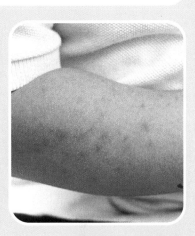

Medical treatment
A short course of steroids relieves severe symptoms.

Outlook
- If sunshine is avoided, rash settles within a few days and disappears within two weeks.
- May recur throughout summer or child may have only one reaction.
- Some children become more tolerant as summer progresses.
- Occasionally 'supersensitive' children react even to winter sunlight.

Looks like
Heat rash (see page 24). Contact dermatitis (see pages 72–73).

Pityriasis rosea

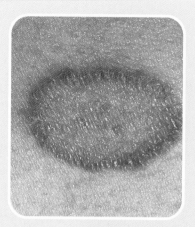

Key signs
Rash of small oval pink patches over the trunk, preceded by a single larger patch of red, scaly skin on the child's upper body (illustrated left).

* Fairly uncommon, rare in babies.

What is it?
A mild condition causing a widespread, usually non-itchy rash. The cause is unknown but is likely to be a virus because pityriasis rosea occasionally occurs in clusters and in institutions. If the cause is a virus, it is not very infectious because an affected child rarely passes it on to other family members.

It is more frequent in spring and autumn. Stress, foods and medicines do not cause pityriasis rosea.

Looks like
Atopic eczema (see pages 68–71).
Psoriasis (see pages 82–83).
Ringworm (see page 53).

Symptoms
- Occasionally, malaise and slight fever, as if the child were developing a cold.
- Red, scaly oval mark measuring 2–5cm (1–2cm) across appears first, usually on the chest or back. This is the 'herald patch' or 'mother patch'.
- One to twenty days later, successive crops of smaller, oval, pink or fawn patches, mostly on the trunk, possibly spreading to upper arms and thighs. Each spot spreads outwards towards a fine scaly outer circle.
- On the back, patches follow the ribs, sweeping down from the spine in a Christmas tree design.
- In children with a dark skin, patches resemble small raised spots that are darker than surrounding skin, with noticeable scaling. They may affect the face, neck, hands and feet rather than the chest and back. Each patch tends to peel from the centre to the outer edge.
- The patches may occasionally itch moderately.

What to do
- Consult a doctor for diagnosis. The doctor can supply a letter for the child's school or nursery to explain that the child is not infectious and can take part in all normal gym, sports and swimming activities.
- Soap and bubble bath can irritate the rash. Use bath oil or aqueous cream instead. Emollient or bath oil will help to prevent dryness.

Medical treatment
Not usually needed. A mild steroid cream can relieve any itching that the child does experience.

Outlook
Pityriasis rosea clears naturally over 3–12 weeks. It almost never returns and doesn't spread between people.

Complementary treatments
Aromatherapy A few drops of camomile or lavender oil in a cool bath are soothing.
Herbalism Aloe vera or calendula cream soothe any itching. Check with your doctor before using herbal preparations on a young child.

Glazed foot

Key signs
Red, shiny skin under and around the toes and on the sole. Deep, painful cracks.

✱ Uncommon.

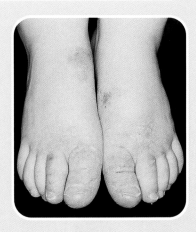

What is it?
Glazed foot (juvenile plantar dermatosis), also known as trainer foot, is a condition in which the skin at the front of children's feet becomes dry, sore and cracked. It can be acutely painful and is attributed to today's shoe styles. Trainers are often blamed, as are nylon and other synthetic materials used in socks and shoes.

Glazed foot does not result from an allergic reaction to a material used in shoe manufacture or colouring. It is not clear whether sweating and friction are important or whether it is more common in children with atopic eczema. The key distinction between glazed foot and athlete's foot is that the latter is itchy

Glazed foot is more common in boys, especially between the ages of four and eight. It is worse in the summer and occasionally affects the hands.

Symptoms
- Shiny red skin under and around the toes, extending to the ball of the foot but not beyond the instep.
- Scaly yellow skin around the sore areas.
- Deep, painful cracks under and between the toes.

What to do
- Use pure cotton socks and sandal-style shoes with open toes
- Dry the child's feet carefully, finishing off under the toes with a hair dryer

- Soften the skin with an emollient before bed.
- Ensure that the child's shoes fit well and that the feet do not slip within them. Buy leather shoes.
- Encourage the child to sit with his or her feet up to rest the cracks.
- Cover the cracks with plasters to speed healing.

Medical treatment
A doctor can prescribe an emollient containing urea or an anti-inflammatory steroid cream.

Outlook
The cracks will heal but this may take some weeks.

Looks like
Atopic eczema (see pages 68–71).
Psoriasis (see pages 82–83).

Psoriasis

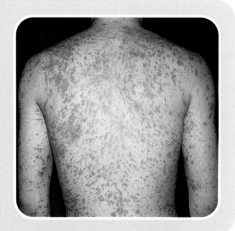

ABOVE: Psoriasis often starts in children as a scatter of small, scaly patches over the trunk and limbs and develops within weeks of a streptococcal throat infection.

Looks like
Ringworm (see page 53). Pityriasis rosea (guttate psoriasis) (see page 80).

What is it?
In psoriasis there is a tendency, often inherited, for the body to make skin cells about seven times as fast as usual. Skin normally grows and replaces itself every three to four weeks, with skin cells dying and rubbing off as they reach the surface. In psoriasis the process is speeded up so the replacement cycle only lasts two to three days.

Spells clear of psoriasis are interspersed with relapses. It is usually better in summer.

There is a family tendency to psoriasis and certain genes are linked to it. If one parent is affected there is a 15 per cent chance of the child developing psoriasis, but this rises to 75 per cent if both parents are affected. Guttate and scalp psoriasis are relatively common in children, although many children have classic plaque psoriasis, the type most commonly seen in adults.

Symptoms
- Clearly edged raised patches of red skin covered with coarse, silvery scales. The patches, which may be itchy, often first appear on the scalp, then the trunk, arms, elbows, leg or knees. The palms and soles are usually free.
- Two to three weeks after a bacterial (streptococcal) throat infection or tonsillitis, a spray of raindrop-like red spots (guttate psoriasis) spreads over the body, especially the chest and back.

What to do
- Liberally apply an emollient such as aqueous cream to the sores to stop them cracking and becoming sore.
- Massage warmed baby, olive or coconut oil into dry skin on the scalp.
- Give tepid baths with bath oil.
- Choose soft, loose clothing.
- Consult a doctor.

Medical treatment
- Treating psoriasis in children means striking a balance between using effective therapies that control the condition and keeping the child's and family's life as normal as possible. Many treatments suitable for adults (including new vitamin A derivatives) are not licensed for children.
- Emollients.
- For children over six, ointments, creams or a scalp solution derived from vitamin D, such as calcipotriol. These are relatively non-staining and non-smelly.
- A tar preparation. Coal tar is both anti-inflammatory and helps to clear scaly skin. It is available as a soap, gel, paste, cream or ointment with calamine (soothing) or salicylic acid (helps skin clearance), in a bandage with zinc (suitable for arms and legs), as a shampoo or, for extensive psoriasis, as a bath additive. Unfortunately, it is messy and stains the skin temporarily brown.

Key signs
Clearly edged, raised patches of dry, crusty skin covered in coarse silvery scales or raindrop spray of red spots over trunk.

** More common in older children, especially in teenagers.

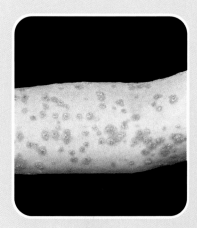

- A preparation containing dithranol as an ointment, paste, cream or gel. Dithranol stops cells growing and dividing and is very effective, but it is messy, stains clothes purple and irritates surrounding skin. Dithranol clears many cases within six weeks and the staining soon fades.
- For guttate psoriasis, the doctor will prescribe emollients, with a moderate steroid cream for severely affected children.
- Courses of ultraviolet B (UVB) treatment are very occasionally used to control severe psoriasis alone or together with other treatments.

Outlook
- Prompt treatment controls psoriasis, but it usually recurs.
- Many people notice that, once treated plaques start to recede, untreated plaques also improve.
- Guttate psoriasis usually clears naturally in a few weeks or months, but children with a tendency to tonsillitis may develop psoriasis with each attack.

- Sunlight heals many people with psoriasis, but it is important to protect your child against sunburn.

Complementary treatments
Check with your doctor before using complementary therapies on children with psoriasis.

Herbalism Apply marshmallow, comfrey or Mahonia aquifolium ointment to the plaques.

Homoeopathy Arsen Alb 6c for thickened, burning and itching skin; Graphites 6c for plaques in skin creases; Lycopodium 6c when plaques are dry and scaly; Petroleum 6c when plaques are rough and itchy, worse in cold weather.

Ayurvedic Tincture of neem leaf has anti-inflammatory and antifungal properties. Traditionally, poultices and pastes have been used to treat psoriasis.

Aromatherapy massage is safe, but it is better to avoid massage on the plaques. Oils that can be used are grapeseed and almond carrier oils.

Swimming rashes

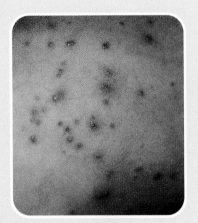

Key signs
Rashes that develop after swimming are usually irritant rashes from contact with disinfectant. The most common is known as 'bromine itch'. Occasionally children swimming in untreated water may contract a skin infection.

* Uncommon.

Caution
A child with a rash of small infected spots which develops after swimming in untreated water, a jacuzzi, hot tub or whirlpool, may have folliculitis, a bacterial (usually Pseudomonas) infection of the hair follicles. This must be shown to a doctor. The treatment is a course of antibiotics.

Symptoms
• Dry, itchy and spotty skin.
• Intense itch within 12 hours of swimming.
OR
• Rash of small infected spots.

What to do
If the rash appears to be caused by the disinfectant, switch pools and choose one that uses ozone or ultraviolet radiation as an accessory treatment, because this allows the disinfectant to be reduced to the safe minimum. This is currently available in a small but growing number of pools.

If you are not in a position to switch swimming pools, moisturize the skin before swimming with a light emollient, possibly using a spray, and shower very thoroughly after swimming.

If an itchy rash develops despite these precautions, treat as for contact dermatitis (see pages 72–73).

What disinfectants are used?
Chlorine is the most common disinfectant and, according to the

What is it?
Skin reactions to chemicals used to disinfect pool water are a form of irritant contact dermatitis (see pages 72–73). As such, they can affect any child but are most common in children with dry, sensitive skin and those with eczema.

UK Pool Water Treatment Advisory Group, there is no evidence that it causes skin reactions when used at recommended levels of 0.5–2 parts per million. The local council or pool owners can tell you how the pool is disinfected and what concentration of disinfectant is used.

Bromine is an alternative disinfectant used in a few pools. Where the bromine derivative BCDMH is used, there have been reports of an intensely itchy type of contact dermatitis occurring within 12 hours of swimming.

Vaccine rashes

What is it?
Immunization with a live vaccine can cause a mild attack of the disease. This is almost always a healthy sign that the vaccine has taken and that the child will develop a strong immunity against that infection. Swellings and redness near the injection site are a local inflammatory response. A rash of non-blanching marks is a type of purpura caused by MMR, as well as by other viral infections. It is rare, affecting only one child in 22,300.

Key signs
Mild, transient rashes of pink or red spots about one week after MMR (mumps, measles, rubella) immunization. Redness and sometimes swelling at injection site after any immunization. Rarely, rash of non-blanching marks after MMR immunization.

** Fairly common.

Symptoms
• Swelling and redness around an injection site are common after immunization for diphtheria, tetanus and whooping cough (DTP), Haemophilus influenzae b (Hib) or MMR.
• Measles-like rash, with fever and general malaise, occurs 6–10 days after MMR immunization.
• The measles-like rash occurs most commonly after first immunization.
• The non-blanching rash of purpura.

What to do
• Give children's paracetamol to relieve discomfort and lower fever. Give a second dose four to six hours later if needed. If the temperature does not drop, consult a doctor.
• Call a doctor immediately if the temperature reaches 39°C (102°F).

Medical treatment
The doctor will give your child medicines to reduce the fever and prevent a febrile convulsion.

Outlook
The child will recover naturally in two or three days from the rash and mild illness associated with MMR vaccine. Any redness and swelling from the DTP vaccine can last for a few days before subsiding naturally.

Caution
In the six weeks after receiving MMR vaccine, children very occasionally get a rash of small, bruise-like spots. This is called thrombocytopenic purpura. Show them to a doctor. A booster MMR dose will only be given if a blood test shows that the child has not developed sufficient antibodies.

Infectious?
No.

Thrush

ABOVE: Unlike milk curds, the white furring inside the mouth of a baby with thrush resists being wiped off. If you succeed, sore red patches are revealed.

Looks like

Sucking blisters (in mouth). Irritant nappy rash (see pages 30–31) or seborrhoeic dermatitis (in nappy area) (see page 23).

What is it?

Thrush is an infection caused by the yeast Candida albicans. Candida species normally live in the body in balance with bacteria and other organisms. Whenever this natural balance is upset, Candida can proliferate and thrush appears. Candida multiplies quickly, causing inflammation.

- Antibiotics can kill the organisms that normally keep Candida in balance.
- Steroid medicines inhaled for asthma may upset the natural environment of the mouth.
- A nappy creates the right environment for Candida to flourish in.

Symptoms

- Vivid red nappy rash that does not respond to normal management approaches or barrier creams.
- A miserable, hard-to-settle baby who pulls back from the breast or bottle.
- Spots inside the mouth that resemble milk curds. Wiped gently with a tissue they may detach to reveal an inflamed sore.

What to do

Check inside the baby's mouth. There are many reasons for feeding reluctance. If you find the characteristic white spots and sore patches, consult a doctor. Breastfeeding mothers need treatment at the same time as their baby.

For thrush in the nappy area, leave off the nappy whenever possible and ensure that the nappy area is really clean and dry. Apply a barrier cream at each nappy change.

Wash your hands scrupulously after nappy changes, and before and after feeding. Keep hands, nails, nipples, tummy buttons, children's hands, bottoms (teaching girls to wipe from front to back) clean. All of these places can act as reservoirs for Candida.

A child inhaling steroid medicines for asthma should rinse his or her mouth and spit out after each treatment.

Medical treatment

A doctor can prescribe an antifungal cream for the sore bottom. The treatment should start to work in two to three days. Apply it for at least a week after the rash has resolved. A mild steroid cream (hydrocortisone one per cent) speeds healing but apply it for one week maximum.

The doctor will also prescribe an antifungal gel or liquid to drop onto the sore patches in the baby's mouth after every feed.

Make sure that the medicine reaches right round the mouth, including between the gums and cheeks.

If you are breastfeeding, you too must be treated. You need an antifungal cream prescribed by a doctor rubbed sparingly on to the nipples and areola after every feed.

If thrush has developed during a course of antibiotics, continue treatment for the full antibiotic course. Do not stop antibiotics to relieve the thrush. If the prescribed creams and gels do not improve the thrush within one to two days, go back to the doctor.

Breastfeeding and thrush

- Mothers report pain after feeds as typical of thrush.
- Breastfeeding should not hurt. If it does, keep asking for professional help.
- With professional support, check baby's positioning for a feed. Your nipples should not be sore and cracked.
- Wash your hands carefully before and after every feed and after changing nappies.
- Change breastpads frequently and wash all clothes in contact with thrush on your hottest wash. Hang in sunshine or tumble-dry thoroughly.
- Sterilize everything that goes into the baby's mouth.
- Treat Candida infection promptly, otherwise it may pass along the milk ducts and infect the breast tissue, causing intense pain.
- Rest as much as possible and eat a nutritious diet. Iron deficiency and anaemia encourage Candida.
- Wear loose, cotton clothes on areas affected by thrush. The fungus thrives in a warm, moist environment.
- Avoid perfumed soaps and bubble baths which damage delicate skin.

Key signs

Intensely sore, angry, red nappy rash. If the mouth is involved, white flecks inside the mouth which leave sore red patches when removed.

*** Very common.

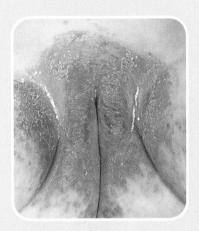

- Thrush can make you give up breastfeeding before you want to.

Complementary treatments

Nutrition The mother may eat two pots daily of live yoghurt containing Lactobacillus acidophilus which help to limit the growth of the Candida yeast.

Homoeopathy Kali Muriaticum 30c at the beginning of an attack; Candida Albicans 30c four times daily for two to three days; also Arsenicum Album 30c when thrush is really burning; Bryonia 30c or Borax 30c when sore mouth makes breastfeeding difficult; Chamomilla 30c when baby has diarrhoea as well and/or is miserable. Give doses every three hours up to four to six doses. Stop or lengthen gaps between doses as symptoms start to improve.

Insect bites and stings

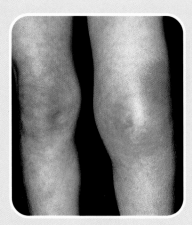

Key signs
One or more intensely sore or itchy swollen spots.

*** Very common.

Caution
Can provoke an allergic reaction and anaphylactic shock. Contact a doctor urgently or, if not available, call your emergency medical number.

Symptoms
- Single or multiple bites or stings.
- Clusters of raised, itchy red spots, especially around the ankles and lower legs.
- Itchy red rash near and around the bites and stings.
- Rash is usually asymmetrical, affecting one side of the body only.
- Frequently only one child per family is affected.

What to do
- Identify the cause.
- Gently remove any sting left in skin by scraping.
- Cool skin with ice pack to reduce inflammation and pain.
- Apply antihistamine cream for additional relief.
- Instruct child to pinch or press any itching spot, rather than scratch. Scratching can introduce a secondary infection.

Medical treatment
- Antihistamine creams to soothe the itch.
- Antibiotics for any secondary infection.

What is it?
Inflammation caused by injection of venom by stinging insect or irritation by components of saliva in sucking or biting insects.

- Very rarely, children develop anaphylactic shock. The doctor can give the child an injection of adrenaline. Children prone to anaphylaxis should carry an adrenaline supply.

Outlook
The rash usually fades within a week. Any hidden source of insect bites (such as animal fleas) means they tend to recur.

Black children can be left with dark blemishes after insect bites, so use an insect repellent.

Complementary treatments
Aromatherapy Apply tea tree oil (for over-twos) or lavender oil diluted in a carrier oil to relieve stinging. First check your child's sensitivity to essential oils by applying a drop of diluted oil to the skin and observing for 24 hours for any reaction.
Herbalism Soothe with aloe vera or calendula gel. Citronella is an effective herbal insect repellent. Garlic eaten regularly may also repel insects.

Plant rashes

Key signs
Plant rashes are a form of dermatitis caused by contact with plants.

✳✳ Common.

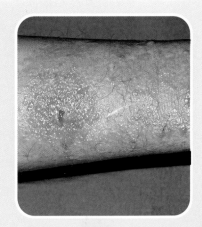

What is it?
Plant rashes are a type of contact dermatitis. The trigger is usually direct contact with part of a plant. Occasionally plant rashes can arise via indirect contact on clothing or from touching an animal that has been in contact with the plant.

What causes it?
In the UK, the stinging nettle (*Urtica dioica*) is the most common plant and causes a transient rash. Giant hogweed (*Heracleum mantegazzianum*) growing by rivers and in untended ground affects unsuspecting children who use the tall stems as pea shooters, trumpets, telescopes or sticks. In sunlight, contact with the sap of cow parsley, wild parsnip and rue, as well as giant hogweed, causes a blistering rash.

In North America, contact with the oil of poison ivy and poison oak (from the Rhus family, no botanical link with English oak or ivy) causes an intensely itchy rash and oozing blisters. Plants in Australia include tar tree, bolly gum and *Toxicodendron succedaneum*.

Symptoms
- Inflamed, itchy red rash or blistering rash on skin directly exposed to plant or pollen.
- Less intense rash follows indirect contact, such as touching clothing that has been in direct contact with the plant.
- The rash usually appears a few hours after contact, but occasionally 7–10 days may elapse.

What to do
- As soon as possible, ideally within five minutes, wash the skin thoroughly using copious water. Removing the sap quickly may prevent a rash developing
- If a rash develops, cool the skin with a facecloth dipped in cold water or an ice pack, or hold under a cold shower.
- Use an over-the-counter antihistamine cream or one per cent hydrocortisone cream to control itching.
- Wash with aqueous cream rather than soap.

Medical treatment
Not usually needed. A doctor can prescribe a stronger steroid cream to apply to an itchy rash or give antibiotics if the rash becomes infected.

Outlook
Plant rashes resolve naturally, but a reaction to poison ivy can take one to two weeks to fade.

Shingles

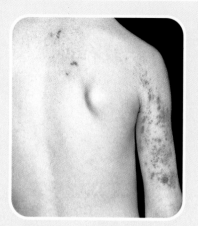

Key signs
Chickenpox-like rash. most common on the chest, back, head or face and limited to one side of the body.

* Uncommon.

Looks like
Impetigo (see page 60).
Hand, foot and mouth disease (see page 44).
Chickenpox (see pages 48–49).

How it is spread
Shingles is *far* less infectious than chickenpox and only by direct contact with the blisters. Covering the rash can prevent someone else from catching it. As with chickenpox, once dried out the rash is not infectious.

Symptoms
- A painful chickenpox-like rash.
- Rash most common on chest, back, head or face; limited to one side of the body.
- Flat, patchy red spots, followed by small, fluid-filled blisters which collapse and form crusts. Successive crops of spots appear and crust over, becoming itchy.

What to do
- Consult a doctor.
- Use paracetamol. Ibuprofen does not work against this type of pain.
- Soothe the burning rash with calamine lotion, a facecloth soaked in cold water, a hot water bottle filled with ice-cold water or crushed ice in a plastic bag.
- To protect an exquisitely painful rash from contact with clothes, cover first with plastic film and dress in soft clothing. Change film frequently so that a secondary infection is not encouraged.
- Once the crusts have fallen off, smoothing moisturizer or vitamin E cream into the skin may prevent scarring.

What is it?
A painful viral condition always caused by the chickenpox virus (varicella virus). Following an attack of chickenpox, the virus lies in a resting state in nerve cells. When re-activated, it causes shingles.

Medical treatment
Medical treatment can relieve the symptoms. An anaesthetic cream containing tetracaine or lidocaine (lignocaine) will relieve acute pain.

Doctors will consider a blood test and precautionary check of the immune system for a very young child who develops shingles.

The antiviral medicine aciclovir is given, especially if the face or genitalia are affected.

Outlook
After two to three weeks the crusts fall off and the rash heals. Shingles rarely causes long-lasting pain in children.

Complementary treatment
Herbalism Consult a health professional before using herbal preparations or creams on a child with shingles. Geranium oil to relieve the pain after shingles; tea tree or Melissa officinalis (1:20 in almond or grapeseed oil) or Melissa cream to help spots clear. Aloe vera with bee propolis soothes the rash. Calendula lotion on the blisters.

Sunburn

What is it?
Sunburn is burning caused by overexposure to medium-wavelength (UVB) sunlight. Moderate exposure to UVB light stimulates melanocytes – the skin cells producing the granules that give skin its colour. After a delay of some hours, overexposure causes redness and soreness, whereas prolonged exposure causes blistering and burning. UVA light damages the deeper layers of the skin, causing ageing (wrinkles). In a high enough dose, UVA can also burn.

In babies and young children, sunburn is almost always accidental. Occasionally it occurs despite the child wearing sunscreen or sunblock.

Symptoms
- Gradually emerging demarcation lines of clothing, with unclothed skin showing red.
- Intensifying redness, reaching a peak 8–12 hours after exposure.
- Extreme soreness.
- Within hours or days, possibly blistering.
- Eventual peeling.

What to do
- Cover the child up completely.
- Remove from the sunshine.
- Give cooling drinks and paracetamol or ibuprofen.
- Cool the skin with wet cloths or dab on aftersun lotion.
- As soon as practicable, give the child a tepid bath, then moisturize the skin with emollients such as an aqueous cream.
- Ingredients of sunscreen creams and lotions can provoke a reaction in children with sensitive skin.

Key signs
Reddened, sore, even blistered skin after sun exposure.

* Not common.

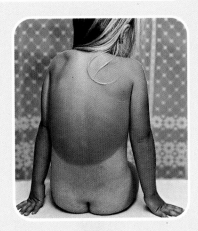

Fragrances, preservatives or a chemical component may be the cause. Change brands. Use a titanium dioxide-based cream.

Medical treatment
The doctor can prescribe a mild steroid cream to reduce inflammation.

Outlook
Sunburn resolves within a day or two, depending on the severity. Repeated sunburn in childhood increases the child's risk of developing malignant melanoma later in life.

Complementary treatments
Aromatherapy Give the child a bath with two drops of lavender oil added. Make up a spray bottle containing 300ml (½ pint) of cold water and two drops of lavender oil. Shake well before use and spray only on unbroken skin.
Herbalism Soothe skin with plain water, with aloe vera gel or juice or nettle lotion added.

Looks like
An allergic reaction to sunscreen.

Boils

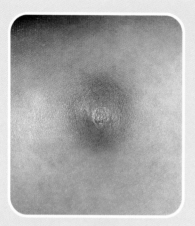

Key signs
Swollen, tender spots, often with a pus-filled centre, caused by bacterial infection of hair follicles.

** Fairly common.

Symptoms
- A sore, red swelling. The centre turns yellowy white, coming to a point when it is ready to burst.
- Small yellow pimples on a visible red flare on white skin. On dark skin only the spot is clearly visible.
- Boils occur most often where the skin is under pressure, such as under a tight collar or where it is moist.

What to do
To ease the pain, lay a warm facecloth over the boil. This may encourage it to burst and ooze pus. Clean by wiping from the centre and pressing very gently around the boil.

Do not squeeze as this can spread the infection. Clean the surrounding area with hot water, pat thoroughly dry and smear on antiseptic cream. Wash your hands. Seal all tissues and wipes that have been in contact with the boil in plastic bags and discard. Cover the site with an open-sided sterile dressing. Covering the skin with an airtight plaster encourages further infection.

What is it?
Boils are bacterial infections of the hair roots usually caused by a staphylococcus. A large, red and very tender lump or smaller pimple develops. The boil gradually develops a whitish yellow centre. Occasional boils are not serious but can be extremely painful.

While the child has a boil, use a shower instead of the bath to avoid spreading infection.

Medical treatment
A child who develops a very large or painful boil or a series of boils should see a doctor.

They make take samples of the infected matter to identify the bacteria and then treat the child with antibiotics.

A doctor may open a large boil with a sterile needle. This does not hurt and immediately reduces the pain, although the area will be sore for a day or two.

Complementary treatments
Aromatherapy Tea tree oil is a natural antiseptic. Do not use on children under two and check first with a qualified therapist. Check also for sensitivity to any essential oils.
Herbalism Taken together, echinacea and goldenseal boost the immune system, but never give for over 10 days and do not give goldenseal to children under two.

Index

Photographic Acknowledgements

Bubbles /Moose Azim 11 left, /Angela Hampton 9, /Frans Rombout 10 bottom /STET 30, /Loisjoy Thurstun 6, 10 top, 17 top, 45 top, 76 top, /Ian West 23 top, 53 top, 62 top, 85 top, 91 top, /Jennie Woodcock 18 top, 19 top, 31 top.

Dr John Buchan Photography 22 top, 28, 44 top, 68, 72, 81 top, 82.

Getty Images /Stone 7, 11 right, /Telegraph 8.

Octopus Publishing Group Limited /Peter Pugh Cook spine, /Gary Holder 35 bottom, 37 bottom, 38 bottom, 39 bottom, 40 bottom, 41 bottom, 42 bottom, 43 bottom, 44 bottom, 45 bottom, 46 bottom, 47 bottom, 49, 53 bottom, 55 bottom, 57, 59 bottom, 60 bottom, 61 bottom, 62 bottom, 63 bottom, 67 bottom, 69 bottom, 73 bottom, 74 bottom, 75 bottom, 76 bottom, 77 bottom, 78 bottom, 79 bottom, 80 bottom, 81 bottom, 83 bottom, 84 bottom, 85 bottom, 88 bottom, 89 bottom, 90 bottom, 91 bottom, 92 bottom, /Gary Holders 87 bottom.

Angela Hampton /Family Life Picture Library 3.

IPC Syndication /Daniel Pangbourne/ Practical Parenting front cover top.

King's College Hospital 12, 13, 29 top, 39 top, 40 top, 59 top, 77 top, 79 top.

Medipics /ICHP 47 top, 67 top, 69 top, 71, 74 top, 83 top, 87 top, /MIG 24 top, 38 top.

Mediscan www.mediscan.co.uk 46 top, 54, 75 top.

Meningitis Research Foundation www.meningitis.org (helpline: 080 8800 3344) 36, 37 top.

Mother and Baby Picture Library /Ian Hooton front cover bottom left, front cover bottom right, front cover bottom centre, 17 bottom, 18 bottom, 19 bottom, 20 bottom, 21 bottom, 22 bottom, 23 bottom, 24 bottom, 25 bottom, 26 bottom, 27 bottom, 29 bottom, 31 bottom.

Dr. P. T. Penny Medical Advisor Amateur Swimming Association pennyswims@hotmail.com 84 top.

Science Photo Library 20 top, 42 top, /John Burbridge 55 top, /CC Studio 48, /Dr P. Marazzi 21 top, 25 top, 26 top, 27 top, 35 top, 41 top, 43 top, 58, 60 top, 61 top, 73 top, 86 top, 88 top, 89 top, 90 top, 92 top, /David Parker 63 top, /Dr H.C. Robinson 80 top /St Bartholemew's Hospital, London, UK 56, 70.

Wellcome Photolibrary 78 top.